Social Protection Floors

Social Protection Floors

Volume 1: Universal Schemes

Edited by Isabel Ortiz, Valérie Schmitt, Loveleen De

International Labour Organization

Cover and back photos:
© Secretaría Técnica de la Presidencia, Government of El Salvador

Social Protection Floors. Volume 1: Universal Schemes
Isabel Ortiz, Valérie Schmitt, Loveleen De (Eds.)

© International Labour Organization 2016, Social Protection Department.
ISBN: 978-1-365-57884-7

Universal social protection is a human right and a State responsibility. As countries begin this pursuit of the Sustainable Development Goals, there is increased recognition that social protection is fundamental in reducing poverty and inequality, in improving human capital and productivity and in supporting growth and jobs. Social protection responds to many of the challenges that we face today.

Guy Ryder,
Director General of the
International Labour Organization

Everyone, as a member of society, has the right to social security.../...Everyone has the right to a standard of living adequate for the health and well-being of himself and of his family, including food, clothing, housing and medical care and necessary social services, and the right to security in the event of unemployment, sickness, disability, widowhood, old age or other lack of livelihood in circumstances beyond his control. Motherhood and childhood are entitled to special care and assistance. All children, whether born in or out of wedlock, shall enjoy the same social protection.

Articles 22 and 25,
Universal Declaration of Human Rights

Acknowledgements

This book is the first volume of the series on "Social Protection Floors" published by the ILO. The editors would like to express their sincere thanks and gratitude to all the people who have contributed to this volume through their authorship, research and analysis. The different chapters of this volume are authored by and benefit from contributions by various people (in alphabetical order):

Aidi Hu, Social Protection Specialist, ILO; Alejandra Beccaria, Consultant for the ILO; Analía Calero, Expert on Employment and Social Protection, Ministry of Economy and Finance, Argentina; André F. Bongestabs, Consultant for the ILO; Ariel Pino, Senior Social Protection Specialist for the Caribbean, ILO; Celine Peyron-Bista, Chief Technical Advisor, ILO; Cristina Lloret, Actuary, ILO; Enkhnasan Nasan-Ulzii, Chief of Social Policy, UNICEF Ulaanbaatar; James Canonge, Social Protection Officer, ILO; Fabio Durán-Valverde, Social Protection Specialist, ILO; Javier Curcio, Researcher, National University of General Sarmiento, Argentina; Joana Borges-Henriques, Social Protection Officer, ILO Praia; Johan Strijdom, African Union Commission; Hiroshi Yamabana, Senior Actuary, ILO; Lkhagvademberel Amgalan, Project Officer, ILO Ulaanbaatar; Lou Tessier, former Social Protection Officer, ILO Yangon; Luis Casanova, National Project Coordinator, ILO Buenos Aires; Oumar Diop, African Union Commission; Pablo Casalí, Senior Social Protection Specialist for the South Cone of Latin America, ILO; Sebastián Waisgrais, Monitoring and Social Inclusion Specialist, UNICEF Buenos Aires; Stefan Urban, Actuary, ILO; Thea Westphal, Consultant for the ILO; Thibault van Langenhove, Social Protection Officer, ILO; Tomas Barbero, ILO; Victoire Umuhire, Legal Officer, ILO and Vijay Gangapersad, Ministry of Social Development and Family Services, Trinidad and Tobago.

The editors also value the support received from various people in reviewing the chapters (in alphabetical order):

Ana Ocampo, World Bank; Anne Drouin, Chief of the Public Finance, Actuarial and Statistics Branch, ILO; Anthony Makwiramiti, Director, Department of Social Development, South Africa; Betina Ramirez-Lopez, Social Protection Officer, ILO Phnom Penh; Catalina Gomez, Consultant for UNICEF; Celine Peyron-Bista, Chief Technical Advisor, ILO; Fabio Durán-Valverde, Senior Social Protection Specialist, ILO; Franziska Gassmann, Professor and Senior Researcher, Maastricht Graduate School of Governance; Gaspar Fajith, Regional Adviser on Economic and Social Policy, UNICEF; James Canonge, Social Protection Officer, ILO; Johanna Sekele, Deputy Director of Disability Grants, Department of Social Development, South Africa; Jurriaan Linsen, Consultant for the ILO; Kagisanyo Kelobang, Social Protection Specialist, ILO; Kathy Kantengwa, The Global Fund; Lucilla Maria Bruni, World Bank; Nuno Cunha, Senior Social Protection Specialist for East Asia and the Pacific, ILO; Roberto Benes, Representative for UNICEF Mongolia; Thaworn Sakunphanit, Director, Health Insurance System Research Office, Thailand; Théopiste Butare, Senior Social Protection Specialist for West Africa, ILO; Thomson Sithole, Deputy Director of Old Age Grants, Department of Social Development, South Africa; Thorsten Behrendt, former Social Protection Officer, ILO; Usa Khiewrord, Regional Programme Manager for East Asia and the Pacific, HelpAge International; Victoria Giroud-Castiella, Social Protection Officer, ILO and Xenia Scheil-Adlung, Senior Health Protection Specialist, ILO.

Last but not the least, the editors express their gratitude to Jessica Vechbanyongratana, Assistant Professor at Chulalongkorn University, Thailand and Victoria Giroud-Castiella, Social Protection Officer, ILO for their support to the series on "Social Protection Floors".

The editors of this volume are Isabel Ortiz, Director of the Social Protection Department, ILO; Valérie Schmitt, Chief of Social Policy, Governance and Standards, ILO and Loveleen De, Social Protection Policy Officer, ILO.

Contents

List of figures

List of tables

Introduction

Social protection floors: A global consensus

Social protection allows for a life in dignity. However, it is still a privilege for far too few. Many older persons do not receive pensions and few children, mothers and persons with disabilities get the support that they need. Too many people are poor and without jobs, left behind by prosperous societies. This massive social protection gap is not acceptable from a human rights perspective. It is also a missed opportunity from a developmental point of view.

Access to social protection is not only a moral imperative, enshrined in the Universal Declaration of Human Rights and other international agreements, but also a critical ingredient for economic growth. Investing for an educated and healthy workforce can foster transitions from low productivity jobs to decent, high productivity jobs. Social protection serves as a stabilizer in times of crisis, providing much-needed income that can maintain or even boost demand and consumption during economic downturns. These positive impacts on workers and the resilience of national economies make social protection systems an attractive investment for many countries and one that will support them in their efforts towards sustainable economic growth.

In a time of rising inequalities, social protection is an indispensable tool for creating inclusive and equitable societies, in which redistribution and solidarity play important roles to build and maintain a lasting social peace.

It is for these reasons that social protection systems and floors are a key priority for the ILO and UN member States. In 2012, Social Protection Floors Recommendation (No. 202) was adopted unanimously by ILO member States (see Annex 1). This Recommendation is the only internationally agreed treaty that reflects a global consensus on universal social protection. It defines social protection floors (SPFs) as a set of social security guarantees that ensure, at a minimum, that all people have access to social protection at adequate benefit levels – or income security. Social protection floors typically include, but are not limited to, cash transfers for children, maternity benefits, disability pensions, support for those without jobs, old-age pensions as well as access to essential health care.

The roll-out of social protection floors is one of the key priorities of the United Nations' 17 Sustainable Development Goals (SDGs), adopted by all countries across the world in 2015. The 2030 development agenda (see Annex 2) calls for efforts to eradicate poverty and equalize income distribution so that as countries continue to develop, the benefits of growth can be enjoyed by all. Specifically, SDG 1.3 commits States to implement nationally appropriate social protection systems and measures for all, including floors, by 2030.[1] By establishing universal social protection systems, including social protection floors, countries can ensure that no one is left behind and that prosperity is shared.

Since the end of the 19th century, significant progress has been made in building social security or social protection systems.[2] From early steps taken in a number of pioneering European countries, the scope of social security, measured by the number of areas covered by social protection systems,[3] was extended at

---

[1] Countries will track progress till 2030 on the proportion of population covered by social protection systems and floors, including coverage of women and men, children, unemployed persons, older persons, persons with disabilities, pregnant women, newborns, victims of work injuries, the poor and the vulnerable.

[2] In this series, social protection and social security are used interchangeably.

[3] Countries tend to build their national social security systems in sequential steps, depending on circumstances and priorities. In many cases, countries have first addressed the area of employment injury; followed by the introduction of old-age pensions, disability and

an impressive pace, including the creation of ministries of labour, ministries of social security and welfare and other relevant institutions. Today, the majority of countries have social protection schemes established by law as well as a myriad of cash transfers, albeit in many developing countries, the schemes benefit only a minority of the population.

Against this backdrop, countries across the world have prioritized the expansion of coverage. From a historical perspective, it is the right time. Today, India is richer than Germany was when it introduced social insurance for all workers in the 1880s and Indonesia is richer than the United States was when it enacted the Social Security Act in 1935. Many developing countries have successfully established universal social protection schemes, providing evidence to the rest of the world that expanding coverage to all is not only necessary but also feasible.

This is because social protection works. It is not a form of charity or a way of giving a few dole-outs to the most vulnerable. Social protection involves strategically designing and implementing comprehensive national systems. Such systems can raise productivity by investing in the workforce; ensure national consumption through higher incomes; and reduce poverty, inequality and political instability. In just a few years, China has put in place nearly universal pensions. Developing countries such as Argentina, Bolivia, Botswana, Brazil, Cabo Verde, Kazakhstan, Lesotho, Maldives, Mongolia, Namibia, Nepal, South Africa, Thailand, Timor-Leste and Uruguay, among others, have established universal social protection schemes. Many governments are expanding the coverage of pensions for older

---

survivor benefits; and the later introduction of sickness, health-care and maternity coverage. Benefits for children and families and unemployment benefits are often implemented last (see the World Social Protection Report 2014-15. Geneva, ILO).

persons, disability and maternity benefits, support for people without jobs and cash transfers for children.

Most interestingly, developing countries are expanding coverage in very innovative ways. We try to reflect the richness of the new 21stcentury approaches in the volumes in this series.

About this volume: Universal schemes

This is the first volume of a series on successful experiences in building social protection floors. This volume showcases 16 experiences from 12 countries which have achieved universal or near-universal social protection coverage in the areas of health care, child allowances, maternity benefits, disability benefits and old-age pensions.

Universal child allowances were introduced in Argentina and Mongolia to support all families with children, reduce extreme poverty and inequality, increase school attendance and reduce the incidence of child labour. While the system in Argentina is composed of three components, i.e. a contributory scheme, a non-contributory scheme and tax deductions for higher-income workers, the Child Money Programme in Mongolia benefits nearly all children and is financed from taxes on the mining sector. Argentina complements the child allowance system with universal maternity protection, which includes provisions for maternity leave, pensions for mothers with seven or more children and access to basic health care and other services.

Due to strong political will, universal access to health care was achieved (or nearly achieved) in China, Colombia, Rwanda and Thailand. The systems are based on a combination of contributory schemes for workers in the formal sector and partially contributory schemes for workers in the informal economy, thereby fostering solidarity and social inclusion. In most countries, extension of coverage was accompanied by gradual improvements in the supply of health-care services. Out-of-pocket payments have been significantly reduced, though further improvements are needed, particularly in China.

In Bolivia, Cabo Verde, China, Lesotho, South Africa, Thailand, Timor-Leste and Trinidad and Tobago, nearly all older persons receive an old-age pension. In addition, in two of these countries, South Africa and Timor-Leste, persons with disabilities receive a disability allowance. Universal coverage was achieved through the combination of contributory and social pensions in Cabo Verde, China, Thailand and Trinidad and Tobago; and the introduction of a tax-based non-contributory benefit covering all retirees in Bolivia (*Renta Dignidad*), Lesotho, South Africa and Timor-Leste. These programmes contribute to reducing poverty incidence among older persons, boost the local demand for goods and services and support political stability. They also benefit other household members especially children, by bringing children out of work and increasing school enrolment. Improvements in equity are needed in countries like China where there are huge disparities between the benefit levels of the contributory and non-contributory rural pensions.

The achievements of different countries presented in this volume demonstrate that universal social protection is feasible. Many low-income and middle-income countries have already started providing health-care coverage to all their residents or income security guarantees to specific categories of the population including children, women during maternity, older persons and people with disabilities. These experiences can serve as a source of inspiration to all countries that have prioritized the development of nationally appropriate social protection systems and measures for all, including floors, as part of their SDG implementation plans. The diversity of examples shows that there is no "one size fits all" approach to the development of universal social protection. Indeed, each country needs to find its own path in line with its vision of society. The number of country cases indicates that there is great scope for South-South exchange in the extension of social protection.

6. Universal Schemes

It is our hope that this volume will give readers concrete ideas on extending social protection to all and, in a few years, many more countries will be able to share their experiences with social protection policy makers from the Global South.

1

Argentina: Universal social protection for children[4]

Since the mid-twentieth century, contributory family allowances have been the main mechanism for providing economic security to children and adolescents in Argentina.

In 2009, the Universal Child Allowance (UCA) was introduced in response to the effects of the global economic crisis, with the aim of consolidating several non-contributory transfer programmes for families with children. This non-contributory cash transfer programme expanded coverage to children under age 18 (and disabled children without any age limit) as well as to unemployed workers, informal workers, domestic workers, temporary workers and social *monotributistas*.[5]

The provision of income insurance for families with children and adolescents is made up of three components: contributory family allowances (CFA), non-contributory family allowances and tax deductions from income (tax on earnings) for higher income workers with children. Together, these three components reach 84.6 per cent of children and adolescents in Argentina. In

---

[4] This chapter was authored by Pablo Casalí, Luis Casanova and Alejandra Beccaria of the ILO, with contributions from Sebastián Waisgrais of UNICEF and Javier Curcio of the National University of General Sarmiento and reviewed by Isabel Ortiz of the ILO. It was first published in September 2016.

[5] Monotributistas are low-income, self-employed workers participating in the Simplified Regime for Small-scale Contributors, known as the Monotributo. Monotributo is a simplified, integrated tax system that rolls income, value-added and social security taxes into a single monthly payment.

absolute terms, some 10.6 million children and adolescents are covered by an income transfer mechanism.

1. Main lessons learned

- The integration of the contributory and non-contributory components is a strategy to guarantee the consolidation of a comprehensive social security system and to ensure the universal protection of children and adolescents, in accordance with the provisions of ILO Social Protection Floors Recommendation, 2012 (No. 202), and the Convention on the Rights of the Child.
- The introduction of the UCA has enabled the development of a system to support the income of families with children, according to the employment status and income earned of the adults responsible for the children and adolescents. The system has three components: contributory component, non-contributory component and tax deductions for higher income workers.
- Studies have shown that the policy to extend social protection through the UCA has had a major impact on reducing extreme poverty and inequality and on increasing school attendance of adolescents aged 16 and 17.

2. Background

Since the late 1990s, several initiatives have been introduced to provide income security for households with children. During the 2000s, social assistance programmes used the presence of children in the household as a reference; programmes for the social protection of children were also implemented at the sub-national level. The UCA was introduced in Argentina as a result of years of intense discussion on proposals designed to universalize protection of children and adolescents. One of the most noteworthy proposals was the extension of family allowances.

The almost universal coverage achieved is due to several factors, most notably the implementation of the UCA, the increase in formal employment that expanded contributory coverage levels and the incorporation of *monotributistas* into the CFA component (April 2016).

Also of note is the extension of non-contributory pensions to mothers of seven or more children, which provides income security to large families (between 2003 and 2016, the number of main beneficiaries increased by 444 per cent).

Figure 1: Social protection coverage of children in Argentina, 2016

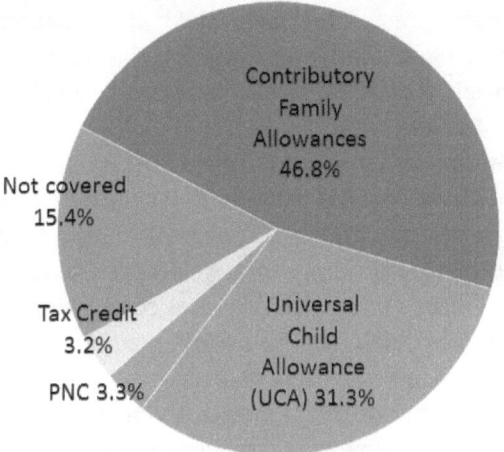

Source: Own elaboration on the basis of data from "National Institute of Statistics and Census" (population census), "Statistical bulletin of social security" and "Nationwide Survey on Social Protection and Social Security".

In legal terms, the UCA was created through a Decree of the National Executive Branch (1.602/09), which modified the Law of Family Allowances (No. 24.714). This decree established the incorporation of a non-contributory sub-system within the General Family Allowance Regime. In other words, both types of benefits are now regulated by this Law.

3. Structure and main characteristics of protection of children and adolescents

As mentioned above, the provision of income security for children and adolescents in Argentina has three components:

- **Contributory family allowances (CFA)** composed of the "Family Child Allowance", which covers the dependents of formal middle- and low-income employees, beneficiaries of certain social security guarantees (unemployment and work injury) and, since April 2016, dependents of workers of the Monotributo regime.
- **Non-contributory family allowances** is composed of the Universal Child Allowance (UCA), which is a semi-conditional cash transfer for each child and disabled child of unemployed workers, those in the informal economy, social *monotributistas, temporary workers* and domestic workers.

  The cash transfer is semi-conditional: 80 per cent is granted through the usual system of social security payments while the remaining 20 per cent is paid once the main beneficiary confirms health check-ups, immunization records and certification of completion of the school year by their children and/or adolescents, whichever is the case.

  The UCA is a component of the non-contributory pillar, together with family allowances for dependents of old-age pension beneficiaries and of certain non-contributory pension beneficiaries (disability and former soldiers in the Falklands War).
- **Deduction or tax credit for each child** for higher income workers who pay income tax. The tax credit is the component available to higher income workers who pay individual income tax.

Low-income beneficiaries of the CFA and UCA beneficiaries receive the same amount, 1,103 Argentina Pesos (ARS) per month. In 2015, the automatic indexation of benefits (twice annually) based on the pension mobility index was established by law.

The National Social Security Administration (ANSES) is responsible for managing both contributory and non-contributory family allowances. In other words, the ANSES receives, processes and evaluates programme applications and pays both benefits.

The integration of the contributory and non-contributory components (CFA and UCA) pave the way for the consolidation of a "comprehensive social security system", as established in the ILO Social Protection Floors Recommendation, 2012 (No. 202).

Nearly six years after the UCA was implemented, evidence indicates that these high-coverage social protection programmes do not have a negative impact on the labour market. This positive result is largely due to the coordination among programmes that guarantee income and promote active labour market policies.

Several factors explain the fact that approximately 15 per cent of children and adolescents are not covered under any scheme. This group mainly includes children and adolescents whose parents are: i) employees with higher earnings – or slightly lower earnings – than the established ceilings; ii) higher income *monotributistas*; iii) independent workers; or iv) immigrants residing in the country for less than three years. The situation of children and adolescents not under family care should also be mentioned given that they are not included in any of the current protection components.

Moreover, there are children and adolescents who are eligible for one of the established schemes but who do not receive benefits for a variety of reasons. These reasons include: problems associated with family relations; problems associated with their or their parents' identification documents; and non-compliance with some requirements for access.

4. Financing

The contributory component is financed through employers' contributions to social security while social security resources cover the cost of the UCA. As a result of the expanded coverage, the resources allocated to cash transfers for children and adolescents have been sharply increased. In 2014, the amount allocated to the protection of this segment of the population was 1.04 per cent of GDP, where the principal components were the UCA (0.50 per cent), the CFA (0.46 per cent) and the family allowances for people receiving an old age pension (0.08 per cent).

5. What are the impacts of the UCA?

Policies to extend social protection, in this case the UCA, had considerable impacts in terms of reducing extreme poverty and inequality. Studies by Bertranou (2010) and Maurizio and Vázquez (2014) show that UCA reduced poverty rates, especially extreme poverty. There is also empirical evidence from studies by Hintze and Costa (2014) and Curcio and Beccaria (2013) that suggest that the UCA contributes to improved income distribution, as measured by the Gini coefficient and income gaps.

Additionally, some studies found that the UCA had a positive impact on school attendance for adolescents between the ages of 16 and 17 (the group with the highest dropout rates), as well as on reducing child labour (Jiménez and Jiménez, 2015). Nevertheless, given the lack of available standardized data, more evidence is needed on the impact of this programme on school attendance, particularly with respect to secondary school.

The implementation of this policy also led to a 50 per cent increase in the number of children and a 14 per cent increase in the number of pregnant women enrolled in the SUMAR Plan, which provides guaranteed health benefits (MSAL, 2012).

6. What are the challenges?

The main challenges for policies to guarantee income security for children and adolescents can be summarized as follows:

- Despite efforts to increase UCA coverage, the challenge remains to incorporate a large number of eligible children and adolescents who, for different reasons, face barriers to accessing benefits.
- The role of established conditions needs to be redefined to emphasize the concept of the "universal right" of children and adolescents to health and education.
- The sufficiency of UCA benefits should be assessed in an effort to enable children and adolescents to get out of poverty.
- A micro-assessment of the UCA should be conducted to identify bottlenecks and propose reforms that help facilitate programme implementation and compliance with established conditions.

7. References

Arcidiácono, P.; Carmona Barrenechea, V.; Straschnoy, M. 2011. "La asignación universal por hijo para protección social: Rupturas y continuidades ¿Hacia un esquema universal?", in *Revista Margen*, No. 61, pp. 1-16.

Bertranou, F. 2010. *Aportes para un piso de protección social en Argentina: El caso de las asignaciones familiares* (Buenos Aires, ILO Country Office for Argentina).

Bertranou, F.; Casalí, P.; Schwarzer, H. 2014. *La estrategia de desarrollo de los sistemas de seguridad social de la OIT: El papel de los pisos de protección social en América Latina y el Caribe* (Lima, ILO Regional Office for Latin America and the Caribbean).

Bertranou, F.; Cetrángolo, O.; Casanova, L.; Beccaria, A; Folgar, J. 2015. *Desempeño y financiamiento de la protección social en Argentina* (Buenos Aires, ILO Country Office for Argentina).

Casalí, P.; Schwarzer, H. 2010. "Social protection floor: Conceptual development and application in Latin America" in *2010 Labour Overview Latin America and the Caribbean* (Lima, ILO Regional Office for Latin America and the Caribbean).

Curcio, J.; Beccaria, A. 2013. "Políticas de protección social y su impacto en la situación de la niñez y de sus familias. El caso de la Asignación Universal por Hijo para Protección Social a tres años de su implementación", paper presented at XI National Political Science Congress, Paraná.

Hintze, S.; Costa, M. 2014. "Capacidad protectoria de la Asignación Universal por Hijo para Protección Social: Problemas y debates a cuatro años de su implementación", in C. Danani and S. Hintze (eds): *Protecciones y desprotecciones II: Problemas y debates de la seguridad social en la Argentina* (Buenos Aires, Universidad Nacional de General Sarmiento).

Jiménez, M.; Jiménez, M. 2015. *Asistencia escolar y participación laboral de los adolescentes en Argentina: el impacto de la Asignación Universal por Hijo*, Working Paper Series No. 11 (Buenos Aires, ILO Country Office for Argentina).

2

Argentina: Universal maternity protection[6]

Argentina's Constitution provides for the protection of pregnant and lactating female workers. Argentina's maternity protection policy is in coherence with the Social Protection Floors Recommendation, 2012 (No.202).

In Argentina, social protection in the case of maternity includes maternity protection in the workplace, contributory and non-contributory family allowances and pensions for mothers with seven or more children. In addition, several programmes provide universal access to basic social services. For example, the SUMAR Programme offers basic health services, including antenatal and postnatal consultations and delivery. The national legal framework also provides paid and unpaid maternity leave and paid paternity leave for registered workers.

1. Main lessons learned

- Maternity protection in Argentina encompasses both transfers in cash and in kind and this makes it coherent with the ILO's Recommendation No. 202. Maternity protection includes income security measures through several social transfer programmes, universal access to basic social services and provisions for maternity leave. Universal maternity protection in Argentina has had

---

[6] This chapter was authored by Analía Calero of the Ministry of Economy and Finance in Argentina and reviewed by Isabel Ortiz, Valérie Schmitt, Fabio Durán and Victoria Giroud of the ILO. It was first published in June 2016.

impressive results; child and maternal mortality have decreased by 34 per cent and 24 per cent respectively.

- The contributory and non-contributory programmes are administered by the National Social Security Administration (ANSES) while complementary health programmes are operated or regulated by the National Health Ministry. Therefore, good coordination among institutions is required to guarantee comprehensive maternity protection.
- The establishment of an adapted legal framework ensures the sustainability of social protection programmes.

2. Towards universal maternity protection

Maternity protection in Argentina encompasses both transfers in cash and in kind. It includes income security measures through social transfer programmes, universal access to basic social services and provisions for maternity leave. In this way, Argentina's maternity protection policy is in line with the Social Protection Floors Recommendation, 2012 (No.202).

3. How is the system organized?

Contributory programmes include maternity protection in the workplace and family allowances. To extend maternity protection to uncovered groups, two non-contributory allowances were established in 2009 and 2011, respectively: the Universal Child Allowance (Asignación Universal por Hijo) and the Pregnancy Allowance (Asignación por Embarazo).

Table 1: Social transfer programmes in Argentina

Programme	Provisions	Beneficiaries
Contributory programmes		
Maternity protection in the workplace	Monthly income replacement equivalent to 100 per cent of the worker's salary	Employees covered by the Law on work-related risks and unemployment protection
Family allowances	Prenatal: between 199 and 2,084 Argentinian pesos (ARS) (US$13-141) per month Per birth: ARS1,125 (US$76) Per adoption: ARS6,748 (US$456) Per child: between ARS199 and 2,084 (US$13-141) per month School allowance: between ARS808 and 1615 (US$55-109) per year	Same as above, plus beneficiaries of the pension system and non-contributory pension, up to a maximum monthly family income of ARS60,000 (US$4,054), set by Law
Non-contributory programmes		
Universal Child Allowance	ARS966 (US$65) per month per child, with conditions on health and education	Monotax beneficiaries, unemployed persons, workers in the informal economy earning below minimum wage, domestic workers
Pregnancy Allowance	ARS966 (US$65) per month from the 12th week of pregnancy through childbirth or interruption of pregnancy	
Pensions for mothers with 7 or more children	Lifetime monthly amount equivalent to the minimum old-age pension of ARS4958.90 (US$335) (ANSES, March 2016)	Mothers with seven or more children (own or adopted children)

Source: Decree 1141/2015-Family allowances from March 2016 onwards.

18. Universal Schemes

The contributory and non-contributory programmes are administered by the National Social Security Administration (ANSES). Out of a total of 13 million children and teenagers below the age of 18 years, the Universal Child Allowance and Pregnancy Allowance cover 7 million, a coverage rate of 53.8 per cent. In addition, income tax reductions are applied to families with children. The combination of the two programmes and income tax deductions brings the coverage to 74.3 per cent of all children below the age of 18 years. At the same time, the National Commission for Social Pensions of the Ministry of Social Development administers the pensions for mothers with seven or more children.

As far as universal access to basic social services is concerned, female workers in the formal economy can access social health services provided by trade unions. They can also access prepaid health-care services in private clinics and sanatoriums. The SUMAR Programme plays an important role, as it provides access to basic health care to vulnerable families with the objective to reduce child and maternal mortality, strengthen access to health care for school age children and teenagers and improve the overall care provided to women through regular health check-ups.

The SUMAR Programme was created in 2012 in the context of the extension of coverage of the Plan Nacer (2005). The SUMAR Programme facilitated access to health care for pregnant women and children up to 6 years of age. It was then extended to children and teenagers of between 6 and 19 years of age, and consequently to men and women of 20 to 64 years of age who are without any contributory social health protection. In 2015 the SUMAR Programme covered 13 million people. According to the 2010 national census, the population without any social health protection was 14 million. Therefore, the SUMAR Programme has contributed significantly to closing the social health protection gap in Argentina.

Table 2: Health services in Argentina

Sub-system	Institutions	Coverage
Public system	Public provincial and district hospitals, as well as primary health centres	Provides health services to the entire population
	SUMAR Programme Essential Public Health Functions Programme (FESP) Remediar and Redes Programmes	Provides health services to the vulnerable population
System of social services	National social services system	Covers health risks for salaried workers and their families
Private sub-system	Enterprises providing prepaid health packages in sanatoriums and private clinics	Provides coverage to those who pay a premium

Source: ILO, Social Protection Platform (www.social-protection.org).

The programme is run by the National Health Ministry and financed from public budget. It is linked with the Universal Child Allowance and Pregnancy Allowance.

In addition, the national legal framework includes paid and unpaid maternity leave for female workers in registered or formal employment. Although there are some differences between the maternity leave policies in the public and private sectors, in both cases the benefits are set at 100 per cent of a worker's salary during the entire maternity leave period. The benefits are financed by social security.

At the end of their maternity leave, mothers can take an unpaid leave called "excedencia" to take care of their child during the first year of life. The unpaid maternity leave only applies to female workers in registered paid employment.

Men are entitled to paternity leave of between two and five days and are not entitled to unpaid leave.

Table 3: Maternity leave in the registered or formal sector in Argentina

Selected measures	Legal protection	Maternity leave	Lactating period
Private sector	Dismissals are prohibited during pregnancy, maternity leave and 7.5 months before and after the delivery date	90 days	2 periods of 30 minutes each until the child reaches 12 months
Public sector	Same rights as permanent staff members (Law on Labour Contract does not apply during the maternity period)	100 days for the 1st and 2nd child; 110 days for the 3rd child and beyond	2 periods of 1 hour each until the child reaches 12 months; option to reach or leave the office 2 hours early or late

Source: Law No. 20.744 on the work contract and Law No. 25.164 on the regulation of the national public employment.

4. What are the main impacts on people's lives?

Over the last ten years, maternity protection coverage was increased and reinforced by linkages and synergies between the various programmes. Due to major affiliation efforts of the SUMAR Programme, 230,000 children have registered for the Universal Child Allowance and, in 2014, 47,000 women automatically received the Pregnancy Allowance.

The existing Universal Child Allowance and Pregnancy Allowance combined with income tax deductions for families with children benefit 74.3 per cent of all children below the age of 18 years. The SUMAR Programme also had a significant impact on Argentina's population by facilitating access to health care for 13 million people. These interventions have contributed to improving the quality of life of the most vulnerable families in Argentina and their implementation signifies substantial progress in the fight against poverty.

The linkages that exist between the Universal Child Allowance and Pregnancy Allowance contributed to an increase in the enrolment of children and pregnant women in the SUMAR Programme by 50 per cent and 14 per cent respectively, in 2014. Due to the extension of maternity protection in the past decade, child and maternal mortality have been reduced by 34 per cent and 24 per cent respectively. The SUMAR Programme has been recognized by the Geneva Health Forum and highlighted as a model and source of inspiration for other countries (Ministry of Health, 2015).

5. What are the main challenges?

One of the main challenges is including the right to care as one of the components of the social protection system (ILO, 2014). Recommendations to ensure that the right to care becomes a reality include:

- ratify ILO's Maternity Protection Convention, 2000 (No. 183), in order to extend the duration of maternity leave from 12 to 14 weeks;
- create the necessary legal framework to ensure that enterprises that employ a certain number of female workers establish maternity rooms and childcare centres, in line with ILO's Workers with Family Responsibilities Convention, 1981 (No. 156), that was ratified by Argentina in 1988;
- promote fathers' co-responsibility in childcare by extending paternity leave to uncovered groups and increasing the duration of the paternity leave;

- improve compliance with the Labour Law through prevention and inspection measures; and
- extend maternity leave to female workers in the informal economy.

6. References

ANSES. 2015. Administración Nacional de la Seguridad Social (Buenos Aires). Available at: www.anses.gob.ar.

ILO. 2009. Protección de la maternidad, Notas OIT sobre Trabajo y Familia No. 4. Available at: www.ilo.org/americas/publicaciones/notas-trabajo-y-familia/lang--es/index.htm.

—. 2010. Maternity at work: A review of national legislation, second edition (Geneva). Available at: www.ilo.org/global/publications/ilo-bookstore/order-online/books/WCMS_142159/lang--es/index.htm.

—. 2012a. Avances en la consolidación de la protección social en Argentina, Notas OIT (Buenos Aires, Trabajo decente en Argentina). Available at: www.ilo.org/buenosaires/publicaciones/notas-trabajo-decente/WCMS_221702/lang--es/index.htm.

—. 2014. Recibir y brindar cuidados en condiciones de equidad: Desafíos de la protección social y las políticas de empleo en Argentina, Documento de Trabajo No. 5 (Buenos Aires). Available at: www.ilo.org/buenosaires/publicaciones/WCMS_302535/lang--es/index.htm.

Ministerio de Salud de la Nación. 2013. Plan para la reducción de la mortalidad materno-infantil de las mujeres y las adolescents (Buenos Aires). Available at: www.msal.gov.ar/plan-reduccion-mortalidad.

—. 2014. Memoria Anual, Programa Sumar, 2013 (Buenos Aires). Available at: www.msal.gov.ar/sumar/images/stories/pdf/memoria-anual-sumar-2013.pdf.

—. 2015. Programa SUMAR (Buenos Aires). Available at: www.msal.gov.ar/sumar.

3

Bolivia: Universal pensions for older persons[7]

Despite having the lowest GDP per capita on the continent, Bolivia has achieved one of the highest coverage rates in old-age pensions. With the introduction of the non-contributory old-age pension Renta Dignidad (Dignity Pension) in 2007, Bolivia closed coverage gaps and achieved universal coverage.

Renta Dignidad costs around 1 per cent of the country's GDP and is financed by public revenues generated from taxes on oil and gas production and dividends from a group of state-owned companies.

The impacts of Renta Dignidad on people's lives are remarkable. For example, the programme led to a reduction in the poverty rate by 14 percentage points at the household level. Renta Dignidad has secured the incomes and consumption of beneficiaries, reduced child labour, and increased school enrolment. In households receiving the benefit, child labour has been halved and school enrolment has reached close to 100 per cent.

---

[7] This chapter was authored by Fabio Durán-Valverde and Tomas Barbero of the ILO and reviewed by Isabel Ortiz and Valérie Schmitt of the ILO. It was first published in June 2016.

1. Main lessons learned

- Bolivia's Renta Dignidad programme shows that universal social protection for older persons is achievable, even in developing countries.
- This non-contributory social protection programme has a significant impact on poverty reduction for older persons and other family members living with them; it has reduced poverty by 14 per cent.
- Political will and government commitment are essential. In particular, increasing fiscal space is indispensable to significantly extending old-age pension coverage. Renta Dignidad is financed by revenues from natural hydrocarbon resources.
- Renta Dignidad is administered by the Ministry of Economy and Public Finance but the Bolivian Armed Forces have also played a critical role in achieving higher coverage rates in remote rural areas. There are over 200 payment points installed in military facilities and its mobile units.
- By boosting local demand, stimulating the rural economy, and improving civil registration in rural areas, the universal old-age pension is a driver of growth and development.

2. What does the system look like?

Renta Dignidad is a universal programme, i.e. there are no conditions or means tests to receive the benefit. Along with the country's conditional cash transfer programmes, Bono Juancito Pinto (for school children) and the Bono Juana Azurduy (for expectant and new mothers and their infants), Renta Dignidad is another step forward towards creating a national social protection floor.

Key figures:
- Renta Dignidad reaches 91 per cent of the population over the age of 60.
- The monthly benefit amount is 250 bolivianos (BOB) (US$35.9) for beneficiaries without a contributory pension. BOB200 ($28.7) is paid to recipients of the contributory scheme.
- Involvement of the armed forces has played a critical role to achieve higher coverage rates in rural areas.

Benefit packages: The monthly benefit amount for retirees who are not part of the contributory pension scheme was raised in 2013 to BOB250 ($35.9) and to BOB200 ($28.7) for those covered by the contributory pension scheme. These amounts represent 38 per cent of the poverty line and 21 per cent of the minimum wage, respectively.

Financing: The scheme's cost (benefits plus administrative costs) amounts to roughly 1 per cent of GDP. It is financed from two sources: resources derived from a direct tax on hydrocarbons and dividends from nationalized public enterprises that are earmarked to finance the Renta Dignidad. The Government's revenue from the exploitation and sale of hydrocarbons has increased tremendously. This in turn has brought about a significant increase in fiscal revenues and hence fiscal space for financing social protection.

Legal aspects: Renta Dignidad was established in 2007 by Act No. 3791, replacing the previous social pension scheme known as BONOSOL. The benefit is guaranteed under the Constitution of 2009, which states that "all older persons have the right to a dignified old age, with human quality and warmth. The State shall provide a lifelong old-age pension in the framework of the integrated social security system, as stipulated by legislation." Eligible beneficiaries must be at least 60 years of age, be a Bolivian or naturalized citizen, be domiciled in the country, and have a national identity document.

Institutional arrangements for delivery: Renta Dignidad is administered by the Ministry of Economy and Public Finance with cooperation from the military and the national banking system in the delivery of benefits.

The pension is paid on a monthly basis. The payments are made in more than 1,100 payment centres across the entire country, including branches of financial institutions and National Armed Forces payment centres. Involvement of the armed forces has played a critical role in reaching high coverage rates in remote rural areas. There are more than 200 payment points installed in military facilities and its mobile units. All military mobile units are equipped with mobile satellite dishes. The centralized database of beneficiaries can be accessed from any place in the country, allowing beneficiaries to collect their pensions anywhere.

3.   How was this major breakthrough achieved?

Consolidation of Renta Dignidad as a universal social pension can be explained by two main factors. First, in the course of privatizing public enterprises in 1995, half of the shares of these companies were sold to foreign investors, while around 48 per cent were granted to Bolivians 21 years of age or older. After the renationalization, the dividends generated by these enterprises were earmarked to finance the Renta Dignidad. Second, in 2006, the Government renationalized the hydrocarbon sector and recovered ownership and control of the country's natural hydrocarbon resources. The allocation of revenues from this sector was renegotiated with an 82 per cent share of revenues going to the State and 18 per cent to private companies. This allowed for the creation of fiscal space for financing social protection.

Figure 2: Cost of Bolivia's Renta Dignidad scheme

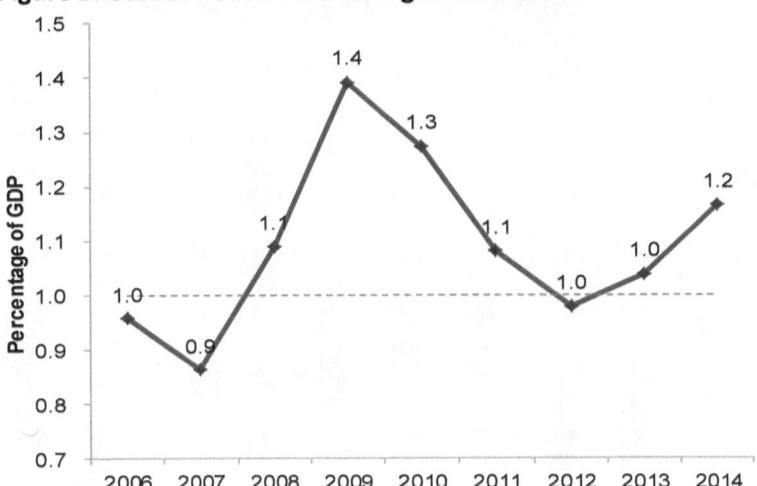

Source: APS. Estadísticas 2014.

4. What is the impact on people's lives?

Outcome: Renta Dignidad is the first, and so far only, universal pension programme in Latin America. The effective coverage rate reaches more than 90 per cent of people over the age of 60.

Impact on people's lives: Renta Dignidad led to a reduction in the poverty rate at the household level by 14 percentage points. The pension stabilizes households' incomes and contributes to boost consumption levels. Positive impacts on child labour and education are also significant. A study conducted by UDAPE (Escobar Loza et al., 2013) shows that children living in households receiving Renta Dignidad benefits are less likely to be working (a reduction of 8.4 percentage points) compared to children in households that do not benefit from Renta Dignidad. Meanwhile, school enrolment rates were 8 percentage points higher in households receiving the social pension, making the enrolment rate close to 100 per cent for this group.

Figure 3: Number of beneficiaries of Bolivia's Renta Dignidad

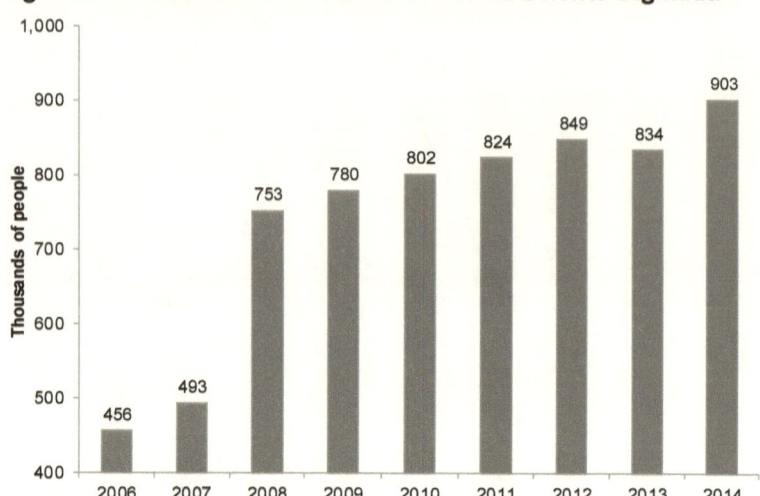

Source: APS. Estadísticas 2014.

Impact on the economy: The impact of social pensions on local development and formalization is well known. Before the introduction of the Renta Dignidad, there were many people of all ages without national personal identification (ID) documents in rural areas. The registration campaign conducted by the programme reached members of households of all ages, including working-age people. The growing number of people with personal IDs and the positive impacts of the social pension on local demand for goods and services in rural areas have contributed to the formalization of the rural economy.

5. What's next?

Bolivia has made significant efforts to universalize its social pension system. The Government is now focusing on improving the administrative and financial governance of the programme, improving the adequacy of benefits, as well as creating complementary linkages with other social protection programmes. Next steps include:

1. overcoming administrative issues to cover the remaining 10 per cent of older persons who are not yet part of Renta Dignidad;
2. maintaining and improving financial governance in order to ensure the sustainability of the programme in the long run;
3. exploring options for increasing the benefit level, which remains modest; and
4. continuing to strengthen the coordination mechanisms with other social protection programmes.

Bolivia's Renta Dignidad is a successful example of guaranteeing universal social protection for older persons. Such achievements would not have been possible without the strong political will and commitment of the Government to universalize the coverage of social pensions and secure financing sources for universal social protection policies.

6. References

Autoridad de Fiscalización y Control de Pensiones y Seguros. Estadísticas. Available at: www.aps.gob.bo/estadisticas/Paginas/Renta-Dignidad.aspx.

Durán-Valverde, F.; Pacheco, F. 2012. Fiscal space and the extension of social protection: Lessons learnt from developing countries (Geneva, ILO). Available at: www.social-protection.org/gimi/gess/RessourcePDF.action?ressource.ressourceId=34168.

Escobar Loza, F.; Martínez Wilde, S.; Mendizábal Córdova, J. 2013. El impacto de la Renta Dignidad: Política de redistribución del ingreso, consumo y reducción de la pobreza en hogares con personas adultas mayores (La Paz, UDAPE). Available at: www.udape.gob.bo/evaluaciondeimpacto/12_Documento_Impacto%20Renta%20Dignidad.pdf.

ILO. 2014. World Social Protection Report 2014/2015: Building economic recovery, inclusive development and social justice (Geneva). Available at: www.social-protection.org/gimi/gess/ShowTheme.action?th.themeId=10.

Ticona Gonzales, M. 2011. "The Dignity Pension (Renta Dignidad): A universal old-age pension scheme", in Sharing Innovative experiences, Successful Social Protection Floor experiences (New York, ILO/UNDP/Global South-South Development Academy). Available at: www.unicef.org/eapro/innovative_experiences.pdf.

4

Cabo Verde: Universal pensions for older persons[8]

Cabo Verde has given social protection a high priority on the road to development, showing a way to combine growth with equity in a context of scarce resources. The country is now one of the most advanced nations in Africa in terms of establishing a social protection floor.

Cabo Verde took two major steps towards a universal pension system: the creation of the National Centre of Social Pensions (CNPS) in 2006 and the unification of pre-existing non-contributory pension programmes. This unified scheme guarantees basic income security for the elderly over 60 years old, the disabled, and children with disabilities living in poor families.

Social pensions in Cabo Verde have reduced the level of poverty and vulnerability of its target population. It is also a concrete step in the direction of establishing a more comprehensive social protection floor.

The social pension covers about 46 per cent of the population 60 years old and over, and the value of the benefit is 20 per cent higher than the poverty line.

---

[8] This chapter was authored by Fabio Durán-Valverde and Joana Borges of the ILO and reviewed by Isabel Ortiz and Valérie Schmitt of the ILO. It was first published in June 2016.

34. Universal Schemes

1. Main lessons learned

- The case of Cabo Verde shows that rapid progress towards the universalization of pension systems is feasible and affordable in developing countries. Strong commitment by the Government is a key ingredient.
- The rapid expansion of pension coverage was achieved by combining contributory and non-contributory programmes.
- The creation of a specialized management institution - the CNPS in Cape Verde- is a critical factor to unify existing programs and keep the strategy on-track.
- Sharing existing infrastructure with other social protection programmes and institutions (post office services, local governments and organizations, and the private sector) allows pension schemes to cover more people and save costs.
- The use of information technology further enables transparent, accountable, and sound management by creating linkages between databases for cross-checking of data and reduction of duplicates.

2. What does the system look like?

Cabo Verde's social protection pension system is the responsibility of the Ministry of Youth, Employment and Human Resources Development. It includes three types of schemes: the non-contributory scheme (social pensions), the mandatory pension scheme that covers both salaried workers and independent workers, and the complementary pension scheme.

The social pensions are managed by the National Centre of Social Pensions (CNPS).

Figure 4: Structure of Cabo Verde's pension system

	Social pensions	Contributory pensions	Complemen-tary pensions (voluntary)
Institutions	MJEDRH: Supervision CNPS: Managment	MJEDRH: Supervision INPS: Managment	Private companies
Benefits	Old-age, disability, survival	Old-age, disability, survival	Private pensions
Beneficiaries	People in poverty, not covered by the contribu-tory scheme	Salaried, domestic & independent workers, & civil servants	People with contributory capacity

Benefit packages: Beneficiaries of social pensions, including the elderly, children and other people with disabilities are entitled to receive a monthly payment of 5,000 Cabo Verdean Escudos (CVE) or about US$65.

The pensioners also benefit from the Mutual Health Fund, which was established to subsidize the purchase of medicines from private pharmacies, up to an annual ceiling of 2,500 CVE. The Mutual Health Fund also provides a funeral allowance of 7,000 CVE.

Financing: The social pensions cost nearly 0.4 per cent of GDP and are fully financed from the general state budget, whereas the Mutual Health Fund is financed from beneficiaries' monthly contributions of 100 CVE per pensioner (2 per cent of the social pension payment's current value).

Legal aspects: The CNPS, created in 2006, manages the social pensions in an autonomous manner. To qualify for the social pension for older persons, applicants must be resident in Cabo

Verde, be 60 years old or above, have an income below the national official poverty line (4,123 CVE in 2007), and not to be covered by any other social security scheme.

Figure 5: Organization of Cabo Verde's social pension system

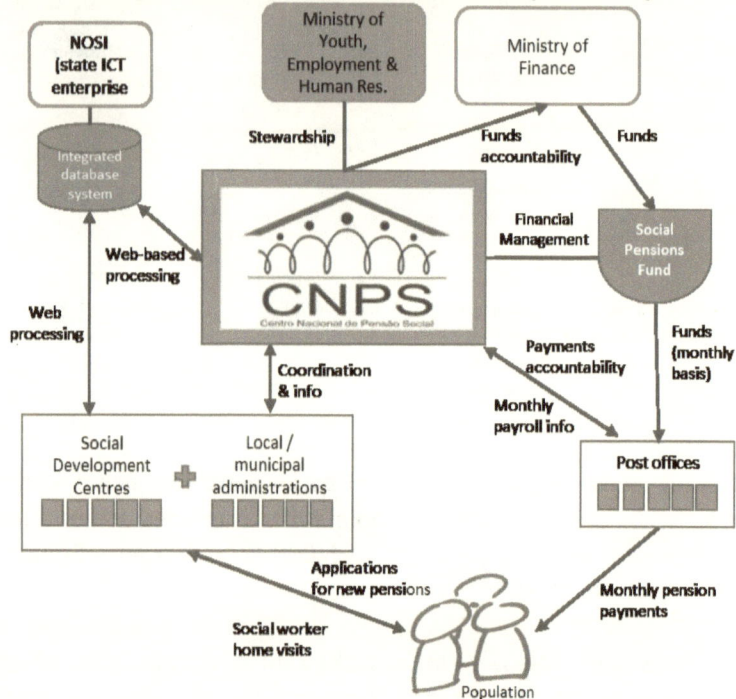

Institutional arrangements for delivery: Social pensions are managed by the CNPS and paid through local post offices every month. The process of claiming the pension starts locally, either through the intervention of Local Development Centres (CDS) or municipal governments. Applicants to the social pensions must complete a form for identification and selection of beneficiaries, as well as provide some basic documentation. Conditions for selection are verified by a social worker through a visit to the domicile of the applicant. The process finishes at the CNPS headquarters with the selection of the beneficiaries. In order to introduce more transparency and enhance governance, a web-based application was implemented to manage all the processes and procedures, thus creating an integrated and consistent database. All ICT functions (software development, databases, and communications) are supported by NOSI, a state company that centrally manages the ICT of state institutions. This feature has allowed for significant progress in integrating the CNPS databases with those of other social protection programmes run on the different islands that comprise the country.

3. How was this major breakthrough achieved?

The CNPS was created in 2006 by merging two pre-existing non-contributory pension schemes. One of the main justifications for the creation of the CNPS was to reduce institutional dispersion in order to increase efficiency. In less than ten years, the social pension almost doubled its coverage by reaching out to women and people in rural areas. Considerable progress has been made in terms of administration improvements since the creation of the CNPS.

4. What are the main results?

Outcomes: Cabo Verde is close to universalizing its pension system. When you add up the contributory and non-contributory coverage, it is estimated that over 90 per cent of older persons receive a pension. According to CNPS, the percentage of the population over 60 covered by a non-contributory pension reached 46 per cent in 2010, among the highest levels in sub-Saharan Africa. In rural areas nearly 74 per cent of people over 60 years of age are protected by social pensions. The performance of CNPS is efficient with administrative costs estimated to be only 1.4 per cent of benefits.

Impacts on people's lives: In terms of coverage, the social pensions have achieved their target. In 2013 more than 84 per cent of the pensioners were 60 or more years old and 69 per cent were women. A large share of beneficiaries is women living in rural areas, which is one of the most vulnerable groups in Cabo Verde.

The amount of the social pension (5,000 CVE) represents about 22 per cent of per capita GDP and is 20 percent more than the poverty line. In other words, the value of the pension is sufficient for a person to cease to be in poverty.

Figure 6: Coverage rates of social pensions in Cabo Verde as a percentage of people over 60 years of age

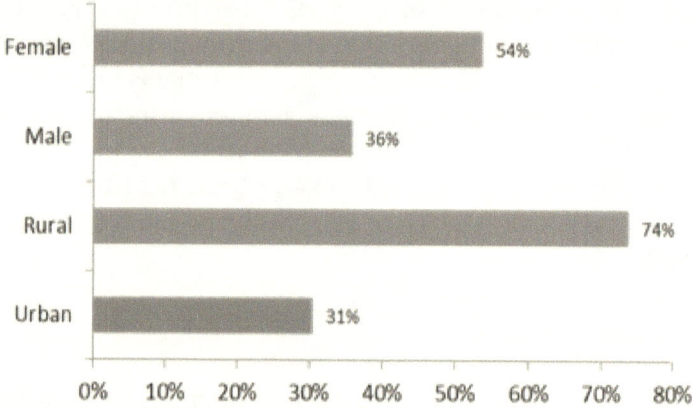

Source: Estimates for 2010 based on CNPS reports.

5. What's next?

Cabo Verde has made significant efforts to extend its social pension system and establish and consolidate its institutional capacity. There are still many challenges to face in order to achieve higher levels of effectiveness and efficiency. Some of these challenges include:

1. Continuing to reinforce the linkages between contributory and non-contributory schemes in the areas of the administration, financing, delivery of services, and tools.

2. Continuing to improve IT and the administrative processes of identification, eligibility, payment of benefits, monitoring and evaluation. Furthermore, an

ideal scenario is that all institutions managing social protection benefits could use a single system to perform those different functions.

6. Final remarks

Cabo Verde moved rapidly towards the universalization of its pension system, providing adequate old-age benefits. Some critical elements that explain this achievement are: the strong political will to finance social protection; the combination of contributory and non-contributory instruments; the unification of previously existing programs and their consolidation into a single specialized institution; the intensive and effective use of information technology; and the importance given to administrative modernization.

7. References

Durán-Valverde, F.; Pacheco, J.; Borges Henriques, J. 2012. A Proteção Social em Cabo Verde: situação e desafios [Social Protection in Cabo Verde: Situation and challenges - SPER] (Praia, ILO – STEP Portugal). Available at: www.social-protection.org/gimi/gess/ShowRessource.action?ressource.ress ourceId=42297.

ILO. 2011. Social Protection Floor in Cape Verde (Praia, ILO – STEP Portugal). Available at: www.social-protection.org/gimi/gess/ShowRessource.action?ressource.ress ourceId=25712.

—. 2014. World Social Protection Report 2014/2015: Building economic recovery, inclusive development and social justice (Geneva). Available at: www.social-protection.org/gimi/gess/ShowTheme.action?th.themeId=10.

Pacheco, J. F.; Durán-Valverde, F.; Lucas, J. 2012. Diagnóstico do Centro Nacional de Pensões Sociais de Cabo Verde (Praia, ILO – STEP Portugal). Available at: www.social-

40. Universal Schemes

protection.org/gimi/gess/ShowRessource.action?ressource.ress
ourceId=31268.

Rodrigues Biscalha, M. 2013. Revisão dos processos para a seleção dos Beneficiários das Pensões Sociais em Cabo Verde (Praia, ILO – STEP Portugal).

5

China: Health care for all[9]

Between 2003 and 2013, the number of people covered by the health insurance system in China increased by ten times and has now achieved universal coverage (96.9 per cent of the population).

Figure 7: Expansion of health insurance coverage in China, 2000-13: Number of insured people (millions)

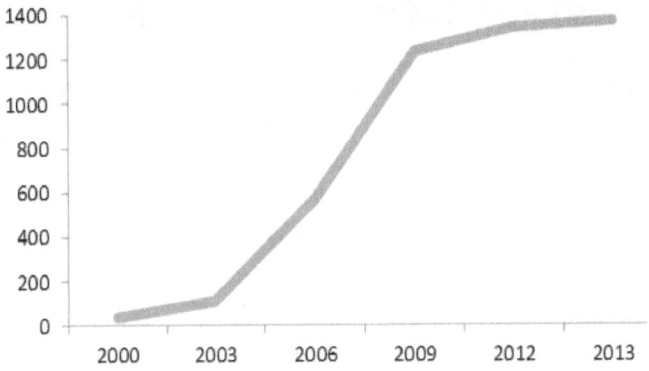

Source: China Statistical Yearbook 2009 & 2014.

The current health insurance system is composed of three main schemes: (1) Health Insurance for Urban Workers (HIW), (2) Health Insurance for Urban Residents (HIUR) and (3) Health Insurance for Rural Residents (HIRR).

---

[9] This chapter was authored by Aidi Hu, supported by Loveleen De of the ILO and reviewed by Valérie Schmitt, Xenia Scheil-Adlung and Thorsten Behrendt of the ILO. It was first published in March 2016.

1. Main lessons learned

- China's experience shows that universal health protection can be achieved in less than ten years.
- Political will and government commitment are necessary for the rapid expansion of health protection. In particular, increasing government expenditures is indispensable for providing rural and other vulnerable groups of the population with meaningful health protection.
- An increase in health insurance coverage contributes to boosting demand for health-care services. It is therefore necessary to ensure that a sufficient number of skilled health workers and quality health-care facilities are equally available and accessible to all in need.
- Introducing cost effectiveness measures and financial incentives to use community-based and other local health services ensures the long-term financial sustainability of the system.
- Universal coverage contributes to social and economic development by enhancing the purchasing power of households, improving the health status of people and productivity of workers, and creating employment in the health sector and beyond.

2. What does the health protection system look like?

Legal aspects: The legal framework of China's health protection system is briefly depicted below.

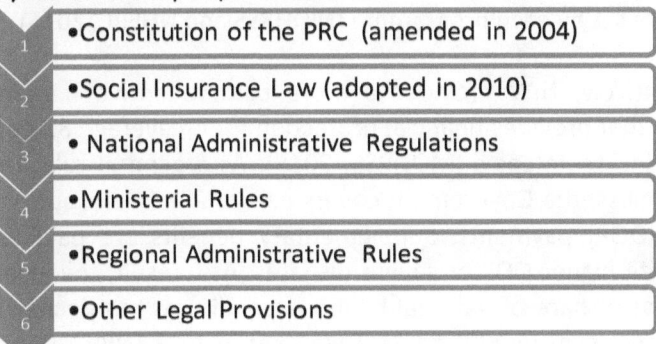

1. •Constitution of the PRC (amended in 2004)
2. •Social Insurance Law (adopted in 2010)
3. • National Administrative Regulations
4. •Ministerial Rules
5. •Regional Administrative Rules
6. •Other Legal Provisions

Financing: The HIW is mainly financed by employer and employee contributions. Employers and employees contribute 6 per cent and 2 per cent of the reference payroll, respectively (MOHRSS, 2015).

The HIUR and HIRR are voluntary insurance schemes that cover 1.1 billion people (NBS, 2014). These schemes are funded by both government subsidies and contributions of the insured. As shown in Table 4 the Government subsidizes a major part of these schemes.

Table 4: Average contribution and subsidy for HIUR and HIRR schemes in China, 2015

Year 2015	Average annual contribution	Average annual subsidy
HIUR & HIRR	CNY 120 per person	CNY 380 per person

Source: MOHRSS, NHFPC and MOF, 2015.

In addition, the Government covers health insurance contributions for poor families.

Benefits: The benefit packages of the three schemes, although different, have all been gradually improved over the last decade. Under the HIUR and HIRR benefit packages, for instance, more than half of the insurable medical costs are covered up to a maximum set by each programme (MOHRSS and NHFPC, 2015).

Comparatively, HIW provides a more comprehensive benefit package that provides financial protection for on average 81 per cent of insurable costs (MOHRSS, 2015). As a general rule for poor families, the Government covers part or all of their out-of-pocket (OOP) payments. Supplementary benefits are paid to those with higher OOP or severe diseases. As a result, the level of OOP as a share of national health expenditures has declined from 60 per cent in 2001 to 33.9 per cent in 2013 (NBS, 2014). The reduction is more striking under the HIRR.

Table 5: HIUR and HIRR benefits in China, 2015

	HIUR (2014)	HIRR (2013)
Benefits as % of insurable cost for hospitalization	70	75
Benefits as % of insurable cost for outpatient care	50	50
Minimum ceiling of annual benefits	6 times the average annual regional income per capita of CNY 60,000	CNY 80,000

Note: Insurable cost is the cost of the benefit package covered by HIUR and HIRR.
Source: MOHRSS and NHFPC, 2015.

Institutional arrangements for delivery: At the national level, the Ministry of Human Resources and Social Security (MOHRSS) is responsible for the global performance of the HIW and HIUR, whilst the National Health and Family Planning Commission (NHFPC) supervises the operations of the HIRR. They cooperate with each other as well as with other related national and regional authorities.

The regional funds of the HIW, HIUR, and HIRR are in charge of the daily operations of the health insurance system. A network of contracted public and private health providers and pharmacies provides the services.

Third-party payment mechanisms have been established between the contracted health providers and insurance schemes. Thus, insured patients only pay their share of OOP after every medical visit. The remaining cost is later invoiced by the health providers to the insurance scheme.

Figure 8: Deficits in effective access to health care in China (2011 or latest available year)

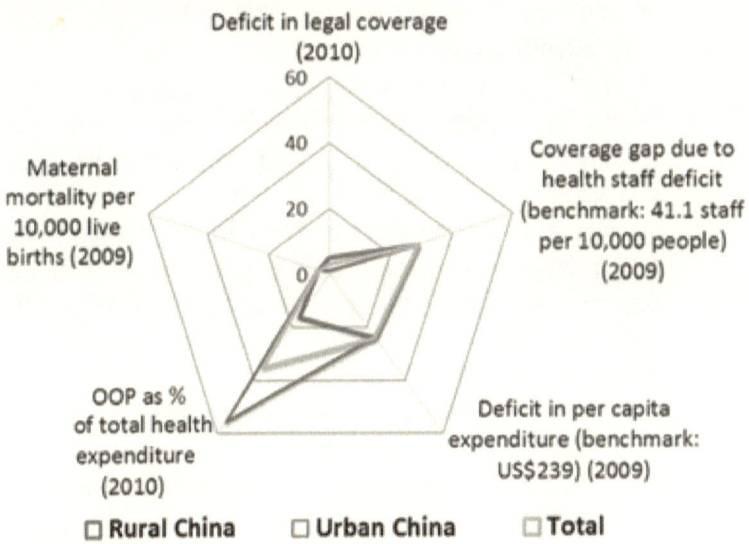

Source: Based on Scheil-Adlung, 2015a.

Access to health care: According to Recommendation No. 202 universal health protection should be based on entitlements prescribed by law and constitute services that meet certain criteria such as availability, accessibility and quality. As shown in Figure 8, only 3.1 per cent of the population was not affiliated to any scheme in 2010. Moreover, the maternal mortality ratio in 2009 was low with only 3.7 deaths per 10,000 live births.

However, access to services was still hampered for some 20 per cent of the population due to deficits in the health workforce and funds. OOP remained high, with a national average of around 35 per cent of total health expenditure and an urban average of 55 per cent.

3. How was this major progress achieved?

A series of events led the extension of health coverage:
- The decision to create a health insurance programme for rural people was jointly made by the Central Committee of the Communist Party of China (CPC) and the State Council in 2002. As a follow-up, the HIRR was launched in 2003 to progressively cover all 800 million rural people (NBS, 2014).
- In 2007, the State Council adopted a policy to pilot a health insurance programme for urban children, students and residents with no health insurance. This policy gave way to the HIUR in the same year.
- "Universal access to basic health care" was set by the CPC in 2007 as an integral part of the national strategic objective to build a moderately prosperous society by 2020 (Hu, 2007). The progress towards universal health protection was thereby accelerated.
- Due to the high level of government financial support to HIRR and HIUR, these two voluntary schemes have helped achieve universal health insurance coverage.
- From 2003 to 2013, the total number of licensed doctors, registered nurses and pharmacists increased significantly from 34.8 to 52.7 per 10,000 residents (NBS, 2014). This increase has reduced the coverage gap due to health staff deficit that is highlighted in Figure 8.

4. What are the main results and impact?

Outcomes: Based on legislation and affiliation to health insurance schemes, universal health protection was achieved in China in 2012 (NBS, 2014).

Impact on people's lives: Universal coverage has enabled more people to seek medical treatment when in need. As a result, the average number of outpatient consultations per person per year went up from 1.7 times in 2003 to 5.4 times in 2013 (NHFPC, 2003 and 2013; NBS, 2014).

Consistently, the national health indicators have improved too. For instance, infant mortality and maternal mortality rates were reduced by 60 per cent and 49 per cent, respectively, over 2000-12. Life expectancy at birth increased from 69 years in 1990 to 75 in 2012 (World Health Organization, 2015).

Impact on the economy: The improved health status of the population has positively impacted workers' productivity. Reductions in OOP payments have minimized the risk of households falling into poverty. Meanwhile, universal coverage has increased the demand for health-related goods and services. This new market has generated new employment and growth. In 2013, the State Council issued a guideline to facilitate the development of these new goods and services.

5. What's next?

Affordability: Despite a gradual decrease of OOP, the level of medical costs borne by insured persons is still considered high, especially for those with low incomes, severe diseases or disabilities. In 2015, the Government launched HIRR and HIUR supplementary programmes for those with severe diseases with the aim of reducing OOP expenditures to less than 50 per cent of the total medical cost (MOHRSS and MOF, 2015). Moreover, there is a significant lack of long-term care protection for older persons as very strict and means-tested eligibility criteria apply (Scheil-Adlung, 2015b).

Availability: Despite reforms to increase and improve the supply side of health care, health services are still overly concentrated in hospitals in large cities. To promote equal access to quality health care, more investment in the rural areas and at the grassroots level is required.

Portability: Patients using health-care facilities outside their region of health insurance still have to pay the full bill first before applying for reimbursement from their own regional health insurance fund. Third-party payment mechanisms should be extended beyond regional borders. Many regions are starting their experiments in portability.

6. References

Central Committee of the CPC and State Council. 2002. 中共中央、国务院 "关于进一步加强农村卫生工作的决定" [Decision on further strengthening rural health work] (Beijing).

Hu. 2007. 胡锦涛在中国共产党第十七次全国代表大会上的报告 [The Report of the 16th Central Committee of the CPC, delivered at the 17th Congress of the CPC] (Beijing).

ILO. 2014. World Social Protection Report 2014-15: Building economic recovery, inclusive development and social justice (Geneva). Available at: www.social-protection.org/gimi/gess/ShowTheme.action?th.themeId=10.

Ministry of Human resources and Social Security (MOHRSS). 2001-14. 2001-2014年人力资源和社会保障事业发展统计公报 [Statistical Bulletins on Human Resources and Social Security Development in 2001 – 2014] (Beijing).

—. 2015. Basic health protection in China, presented at a tripartite seminar on Social Security (Minimum Standards) convention, Zhenjiang.

—; Ministry of Finance (MOF). 2015. 人社部、财政部"关于做好2015年城镇居民基本医疗保险工作的通知 [Notices on the implementation of the HIUR in 2015] (Beijing).

National Bureau of Statistics (NBS). 2009, 2014. 中国统计年鉴 2009, 2014 [China Statistical Yearbook] (Beijing).

National Health and Family Planning Commission (NHFPC). 2003, 2014. 2003年中国卫生事业发展情况统计公报, 2013年卫生和计划生育事业发展统计公报 [Statistic Bulletin on Health Development in 2003, Statistic Bulletin on the Development of Health and Family Planning in 2013] (Beijing).

—. 2015. Management and development of the HIRR, presented at a tripartite seminar on Social Security (Minimum Standards) convention, Zhenjiang.

—; MOF. 2015. 国家卫生计生委, 财政部"关于做好2015年新型农村合作医疗工作的通知" [Notice on the implementation of the HIRR in 2015] (Beijing).

Scheil-Adlung, X (ed.). 2015a. ESS Document No. 47: Global evidence on inequities in rural health protection (Geneva).

—. 2015b. ESS Working Paper No. 50: Long-term care protection for older persons: A review of coverage deficits in 46 countries (Geneva).

State Council. 2007. 国务院"关于开展城镇居民基本医疗保险试点的指导意见" [Guidance on piloting the HIUR] (Beijing).

50. Universal Schemes

一.   2013.   国务院关于促进健康服务业发展的若干意见 [Guideline on the promotion of health-related industries] (Beijing).

World Health Organization. 2015. World Health Statistics 2014 (Geneva).

6

China: Universal pensions[10]

Between 2009 and 2013, China tripled the number of people covered by the old-age pension system, making impressive progress in achieving its goal of universal coverage by 2020.

Figure 9: Expansion of pension coverage in China, 2001-13

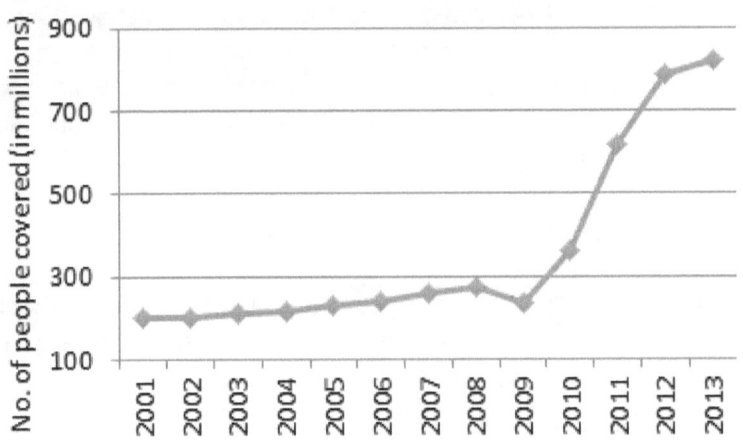

Source: Annual statistical bulletins on human resources and social security development (ASB), 2001-2013.

---

[10] This chapter was authored by Aidi Hu of the ILO and reviewed by Isabel Ortiz, Valérie Schmitt and Jurriaan Linsen of the ILO. It was first published in May 2015.

1. Main lessons learned

- The Chinese experience shows that universality can be achieved by combining contributory schemes and non-contributory social pensions, in line with the Social Protection Floors Recommendation, 2012 (No. 202).
- Extending pension coverage to all citizens within a very short period is feasible.
- Political will and government commitment is essential. In particular, increasing government expenditure is indispensable for covering vulnerable groups that have no or limited capacity to pay contributions.
- Universal pensions, as part of social protection floors, increase domestic consumption and demand, promote human development and social stability, all of which are fundamental for national development and economic growth.

2. What does the pension system look like?

Overall structure: The current state pension system consists of three schemes: (1) an urban workers' pension, (2) a civil servants' pension, and (3) a residents' pension - for those rural and urban residents not covered under the first two.

Benefits and financing: Upon retirement, urban workers receive a state pension consisting of two components: a solidarity component (SC) financed by employers' contributions (accounts for about 20 per cent of payroll) and an individual pension component (IP) calculated based on a worker's accumulated contributions, where contributions are 8 per cent of a worker's reference income. The urban workers' pension scheme consists of hundreds of sub-schemes run independently by local authorities, with some sub-schemes in surplus and others in deficit. To secure full and on-time payments of current pensions, the Government supplements many of these sub-schemes.

Until October 2014, retired civil servants received a single state pension based on their pre-retirement salaries and the number of years of service, paid directly out of the government unit budgets. The scheme is currently being converted into a social insurance pension with two components similar to the urban workers' pension: an SC funded by employers' contributions and an IP funded by employees' contributions. It remains to be seen whether it will become a single nationwide scheme.

The residents' pension also consists of two components. The SC is entirely financed by the Government. The IP is financed by contributions of the insured as well as some government subsidies. However, the majority of the current generation of pensioners only receive the SC component as they had already exceeded the pensionable age when the scheme was introduced. Unlike the other two schemes, participation in the residents' pension is voluntary. The scheme is also composed of many independent locally run sub-schemes.

Legal aspects: The legal framework of the pension system can be depicted as follows:

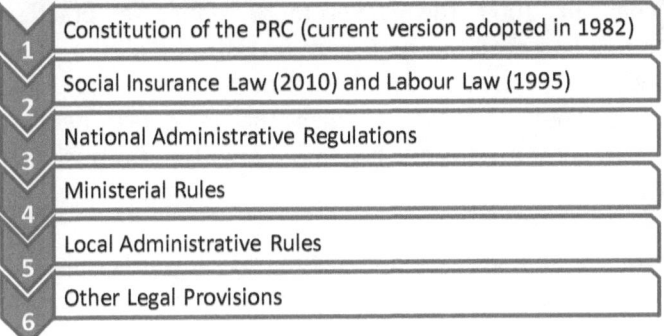

1. Constitution of the PRC (current version adopted in 1982)
2. Social Insurance Law (2010) and Labour Law (1995)
3. National Administrative Regulations
4. Ministerial Rules
5. Local Administrative Rules
6. Other Legal Provisions

Institutional arrangements for delivery: The pension schemes are managed by local social insurance institutions. Contributions are collected by social insurance agencies or by tax authorities. Pensions are paid directly to beneficiaries' designated bank accounts.

3. How was this major breakthrough achieved?

Landmarks: The following events mark the extension of pension coverage since 2009:

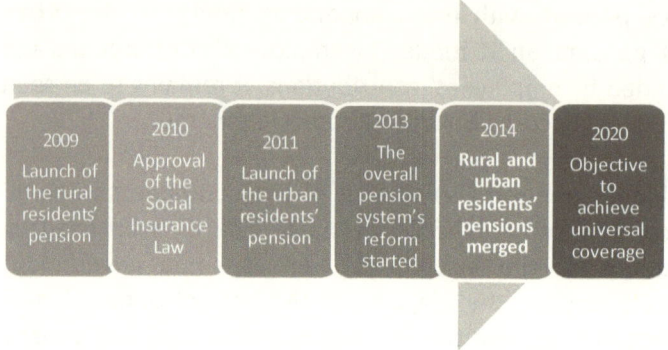

Strong political will: Extending old age pensions to all was driven by a strong commitment to reduce poverty and inequality, and to sustain economic development. Taking the rural pension as a concrete example, the 16th and 17th National Congress of the Communist Party called for the development of an old-age pension for the rural population in 2002 and 2006, respectively. In 2009 the Government issued a practical Guidance and launched the rural pension with the aim to cover the entire rural population by 2020. It merged with the urban residents' pension in 2014 to form the residents' pension scheme. The other pension systems benefited from similar political support.

Administrative and social support: Progress towards universal coverage has also been the result of strong leadership by the central Government and active development of new programme initiatives by local governments. Effective innovative initiatives were often taken up as national policy and implemented across the country. Also, the All China Federation of Trade Unions played an important role in the extension of pension coverage.

Fiscal support: All three schemes benefit from public subsidies. With regards to the residents' pension, a large proportion of its total pension expenditures is supported by government contributions. Revenue sources for the residents' pension in 2013 are as follows:

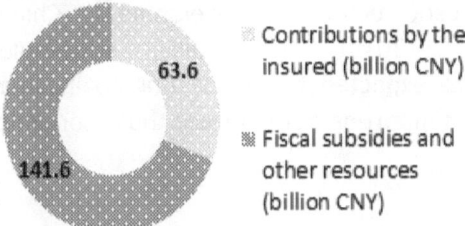

Contributions by the insured (billion CNY)

Fiscal subsidies and other resources (billion CNY)

Source: ASB, 2013.

4. What are the main developmental results and impact on people's lives?

To build a harmonious society is one of the core objectives of the Chinese government. The 12th Five Year Plan launched in 2011 also aimed at increasing aggregate demand by a number of measures such as more public spending on social protection and public services, higher minimum wages and reducing the savings rate of households.

Impact on people's lives: By the end of 2013, about 80 per cent of the population in working age and above, regardless of their employment and contribution histories, were covered under the pension system (MOHRSS, 2013). Civil servants have long enjoyed relatively high benefit levels. The benefits paid under the workers' pension have steadily increased at an annual rate of 10 per cent over the last eleven years, generally ensuring a decent life for these pensioners (Wen, 2014). Although the residents' pension benefit level is still far from adequate, it undoubtedly helps many older people who live in vulnerable conditions.

Impact on the economy: The increases in both the pension coverage and benefit levels have enhanced the purchasing power of people in old age. Since pensioners represent a large and growing component of Chinese society, domestic consumption and markets targeting older persons—such as customised foods, clothing, health, medicine, care, and tourism—have rapidly developed and expanded, forming new opportunities for domestic economic development (China Consumers' Association, 2013). Additionally, household precautionary savings are expected to reduce due to income security and health care, supporting demand and thus economic growth.

5. What's next?

The Government is continuing the expansion of pensions and further improving the system's adequacy, sustainably, and equity.

Benefit adequacy. In particular, there are concerns about the low level of benefits paid to 130.7 million pensioners under the residents' pension. On average, the benefits paid represent less than 11 per cent of average income per capita in rural areas in 2012 (National Bureau of Statistics of People's Republic of China (NBOS), 2013; MOHRSS, 2012), much lower than the minimum standard set in the Social Security (Minimum Standards) Convention, 1952 (No. 102).

Sustainability: China's economic growth, measured at around 10 per cent annually for three decades, has slowed recently to just over 7 per cent. At the same time, the aging of China's population is accelerating as a consequence of the baby-boom in 1950s and 1960s, the implementation of the one-child policy, and constant improvements in life expectancy. Though China has significant fiscal space for social protection, it is contemplating and developing policy measures to ensure the long-term economic sustainability of the pension system, such as increasing the pensionable age.

Equity: Benefit level disparities exist among and within the three schemes. As illustrated in the figure below, the ratio of average benefits in 2013 was estimated to be 100:51:2 for civil servants' pension, workers' pension, and residents' pension respectively.

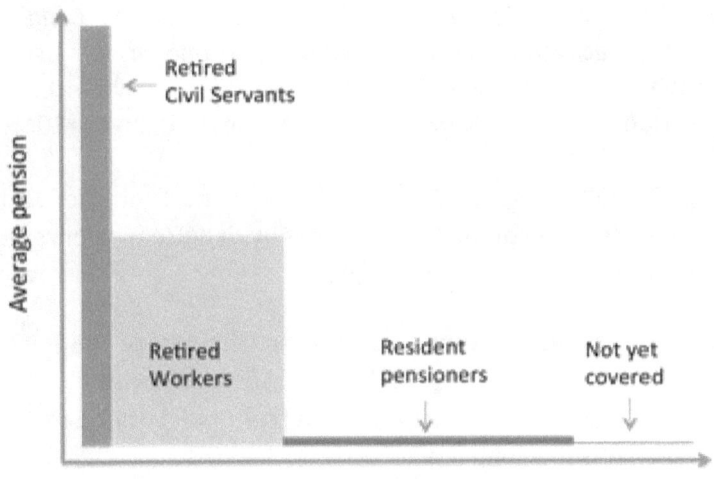

Source: Based on ILO estimates and MOHRSS, 2001-13.

Within the workers' pension scheme, there are regional disparities in the pension replacement rates. For instance, in 2012 the average replacement rate was 70.5 per cent in Shandong, but only 43.2 per cent in Chongqing (Zheng, 2013).

Overall, the phenomenal progress in expanding pension coverage is being continued, fast-tracking universal pension coverage by 2020, in line with the Social Protection Floors Recommendation, 2012 (No. 202).

6. References

Central Committee of the Communist Party of China (CPC). 2006. 中共中央关于构建社会主义和谐社会若干重大问题的决定 [Resolution on a number of important issues for building up a socialist harmonious society] (Beijing).

China Consumers' Association. 2013. 2013年中国老年消费者权益保护调查报告 [Survey report on the protection of old-age consumers' rights and interest in 2013] (Beijing).

ILO. 2014. *World Social Protection Report 2014-15: Building economic recovery, inclusive development and social justice* (Geneva). Available at: www.social-protection.org/gimi/gess/ShowTheme.action?th.themeId=10.

Jiang, Z. 2002. "党的十六大报告" [The Report of the 15th Central Committee of the CPC], address by Jiang Zemin delivered at its 16th National Congress (Beijing).

Ministry of Human Resources and Social Security of the P.R.C. 2001-13.人力资源和社会保障事业发展统计公 [Annual Statistical Bulletins on Human Resources and Social Security Development] (Beijing).

National Bureau of Statistics of People's Republic of the P.R.C. 2013-14. 中国统计年鉴 [China Statistical Yearbook] (Beijing).

State Council. 2009. 国务院关于开展新型农村 社会养老保险试点的指导意见 [Guidance on piloting and setting up a new rural social insurance pension system] (Beijing).

Wen, R. 2015. "中国连续十年提高企退人员养老金 翻1.7倍人均近2千" [Workers' pension has increased consecutively over the past 10 years, reaching nearly 2000 CNY per retiree per month on average, about 1.7 times higher than its level in 2004], in *New Beijing Daily* (Beijing), 9 Jan.

Zheng, B. 2013. "养老金待遇省际差距日益凸显 替代率最高相差27%" [The disparity in pension replacement rate among regions is growing with as high as 27 percentage points' difference], in *Shebao Wang* [China Social Security Net] (Beijing), 26 Sep.

7

Colombia: Progress towards universal health protection[11]

After two decades of development, the Colombian health insurance system exhibits very positive results. It is estimated that the rate of affiliation to the social health insurance schemes rose from 25 per cent in 1993 before the reforms to 96 per cent in 2014.

Out-of-pocket expenditures (OOP) fell to 15.9 per cent of national total health expenditures in 2011 (MSPS, 2014). According to the ILO's World Social Protection Report 2014/2015, per capita health expenditure not financed by OOP reached 358.5 US$ and the share of live births attended by skilled health staff reached 99.2 per cent. Hence, Colombia is one of the most notable cases of recent progress in health protection in Latin America.

1. Main lessons learned

- Significant progress towards universal health protection is feasible and affordable for developing countries.
- Colombia's FOSIGA solidarity and guarantee fund played a critical role in pooling funds from different sources and linking contributory and non-contributory schemes.
- The creation of a single set of health services through the Mandatory Health Plan (POS), contributed to

---

[11] This chapter was authored by Fabio Durán-Valverde of the ILO and reviewed by Isabel Ortiz, Valérie Schmitt and Xenia Scheil-Adlung of the ILO. It was first published in November 2014.

standardizing benefits across all insurers and providers, public and private.

- It is possible to obtain highly successful results in terms of expansion of health coverage to rural populations and reduction of out-of-pocket expenditure payments by families.
- The political economy of structural health reform is highly complex and may generate divergent views between stakeholders. Therefore, social dialogue is essential.

Figure 10: Health protection system in Colombia

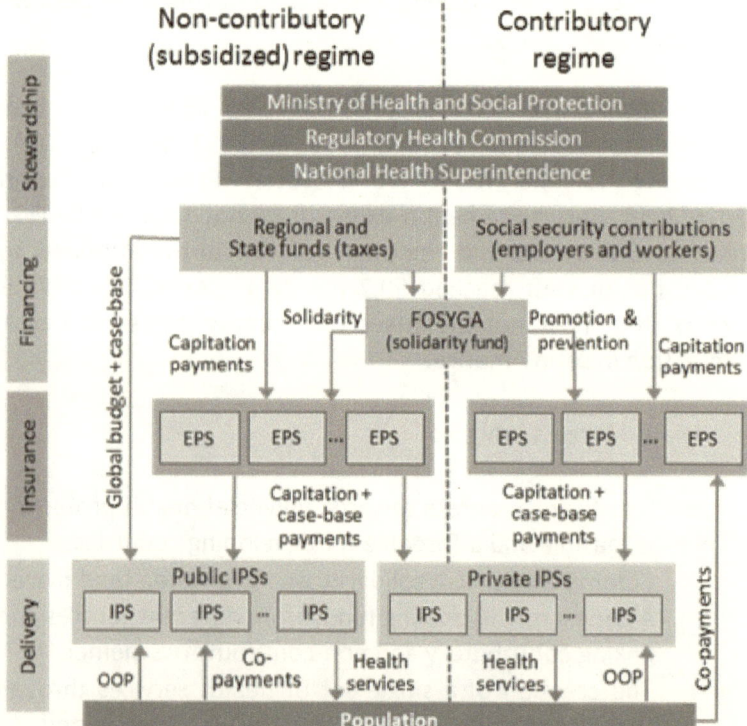

Source: Adapted from Vargas et al, 2010.

2. What does the system look like?

The Colombian health system is based on the principle of "universality", which means that all citizens are obliged to join one of two insurance schemes: a contributory plan for employees and self-employed workers with contributory capacity or a subsidized (non-contributory) scheme for informal workers and low-income self-employed workers (see Figure 10).

Benefit packages: Members, either in the subsidized or the contributory scheme, are entitled to the same benefits. A single service package is defined by the Mandatory Health Plan (POS), which is composed of interventions aimed at health promotion, prevention, and medical care services, including pharmaceutical drugs for members and their families. The POS also includes cash benefits in case of illness and maternity leave. Public and private Health Promotion Entities (EPS), in their role as insurers, are responsible for ensuring citizens have access to POS entitlements.

Financing: The Contributory Scheme is financed by compulsory contributions from employers, employees, the self-employed, and pensioners. Participants contribute according to their payment capacity. The Subsidized Scheme is financed by taxes and transfers from the Contributory Scheme. A per capita payment to deliver the POS —the Capitation Payment Unit (UPC) — is transferred by the Government to the Health Promotion Entities according to the number of enrolled members in each EPS. Thus, EPSs compete for the enrolment of new members in order to maximize their revenue. A Solidarity and Guarantee Fund (FOSYGA) was created to provide cross-subsidies between schemes and finances promotion and prevention interventions.

Legal aspects: The health system was created in 1993 by Law 100. Several reforms have been introduced over time in order to correct problems. In 2007, the Government approved a legal reform to improve stewardship functions, the financing, the financial balance, and the quantity and quality of current services. In 2011, further reforms were introduced to create a single POS for all residents (the former POS provided lower standards for the Subsidized Regime), reach universal coverage, and ensure territorial portability of benefits. Other reforms are currently under debate and highlight the divergent views on the health system among stakeholders. An element of concern is the increasing "judicialization" of the system, whereby the constitutional court has adopted several resolutions to guarantee to the whole population effective access to the POS.

Institutional arrangements for delivery: EPS insurers in the contributory and subsidized schemes purchase services from health provider institutions (IPS), which may be either public or private entities. Public hospitals became State-owned social corporations with legal personality, equity capital, and administrative autonomy. Thus, the system has public and private provision of health-care services. Regulation and oversight of health insurers and providers is under the responsibility of a public entity called SuperSalud. Only people identified through SISBEN, a system for identifying social assistance beneficiaries, are entitled to non-contributory coverage (subsidized scheme).

3. How was this progress achieved?

The current situation of the Colombian health system is the result of a long process of major structural reforms led by the Government with both proponents and opponents. Reforms involved the discontinuation or transformation of old social insurance institutions. One of the more debated topics among stakeholders is the importance given to the private sector in the newly managed competition model. Critics of private participation in health care provision and insurance functions insist on the high intermediation costs generated by private insurers (financial intermediation costs, excessive profits, etc.) as well as the problems of lack of competition, low quality of services, and patient refusal. Proponents highlight the results so far achieved: the strong expansion of coverage increased supply of health services, and the commitment of the Government in financing health for the low-income population.

4. What are the main impacts?

Outcomes: High levels of affiliation (coverage) rates achieved by the Colombian social health insurance system have had positive implications for the well-being of the population. OOP fell dramatically from 43.7 per cent of national health expenditures in 1993 to 15.9 per cent in 2011 (MSPS, 2014), generating a considerable reduction in vulnerability for many Colombians. Thanks to the strong expansion in financing, total health expenditures financed with public resources reached 73.8 per cent in 2011 (MSPS, 2014), one of the highest rates in Latin America.

Impacts on people's lives: One of the most remarkable achievements of Colombia is the extension of health protection and effective access to health services to rural and poor populations. Several studies now show significant increases in the use of health services in rural areas. As a result, since the introduction of the health care reform in 1993, the number of infant and maternal deaths has fallen by 40 per cent and prenatal care has increased by 17 percentage points, with significant improvements in immunization rates for children under the age of 2, according to World Bank figures.

Impacts on the economy: It is recognized that investments in the health sector generate multiplier effects and linkages with other economic sectors. For example, medical tourism is a developing industry in Colombia as a result of the sustained increase in the quality of medical services.

5. What's next?

Despite its accomplishments, the Colombian health system is not free of problems and criticisms, including divergent views on the direction of future reforms. Among the many challenges that remain to be addressed are:

- Complete universal access to health protection and effectively equalize the POS across schemes.
- Close the gaps in the availability of health care particularly in rural areas through the provision of a sufficient number of health workers to ensure that all in need have effective access to quality health care.
- Enhance efficiency and effectiveness of the overall health system
- Improve scope and quality of health services and reduce denial of treatment by insurance companies.
- Strengthen social dialogue as a part of the current model.
- Increase membership in the contributory scheme in order to enhance fiscal sustainability through increased social contributions.
- Improve national health account data and quality of information on health in order to strengthen government monitoring, planning and decision-making capabilities.
- Improve the procedures for beneficiaries to appeal in case of denial of treatment, in order to reduce the use of the constitutional channel to appeal.
- Reduce intermediation costs generated by EPSs.
- Improve the regulatory framework and increase regulatory capacity of the State.

6. References

Agudelo, C. et al. 2011. "Sistema de salud en Colombia: 20 años de logros y problemas", in Ciência & Saúde Coletiva, Vol. 16, No. 6, pp. 2817-2828. Available at: www.scielosp.org/pdf/csc/v16n6/20.pdf.

Castañeda, C. et al. 2012. La sostenibilidad financiera del sistema de salud colombiano: Dinámica del gasto y principales retos de cara al futuro (Bogota, Fedesarrollo). Available at: www.fedesarrollo.org.co/wp-content/uploads/2011/08/La-sostenibilidad-financiera-del-Sistema-de-Salud-Colombiano-Libro-Sura-Final-20121.pdf.

CEPAL. 2013. "Tendencias recientes del gasto social dentro del gasto público y del gasto de los hogares en salud", in Panorama Social 2013 (Santiago). Available at: www.cepal.org/publicaciones/xml/9/51769/CapituloV.pdf

Durán, J.; Uprimny, R. 2014. "La judicialización de la salud en Colombia: El desafío de lograr los consensos hacia mayor equidad y cobertura universal", in Pactos sociales para una protección social más inclusiva: Experiencias, obstáculos y posibilidades en América Latina y Europa (Santiago, CEPAL/Cooperación Alemana). Available at: www.cepal.org/publicaciones/xml/1/52951/PactossocialesparaProteccionSocial.pdf

ILO. 2014. World Social Protection Report 2014/2015. Building economic recovery, inclusive development and social justice (Geneva). Available at: www.social-protection.org/gimi/gess/ShowTheme.action?th.themeId=10

MSPS. 2014. Cifras financieras del sector salud. Gasto en salud Colombia 2004-2011. Boletín Bimestral No.2 Enero-Febrero 2014 (Bogotá). Available at: www.minsalud.gov.co/sites/rid/Lists/BibliotecaDigital/RIDE/VP/FS/Cifras%20financieras%20del%20Sector%20Salud%20-%20Bolet%C3%ADn%20No%202.pdf

Scheil-Adlung, Xenia. 2014. Universal Health Protection: Progress to date and the way forward. Paper 10. Social Protection Policy Papers (Geneva). Available at: www.ilo.org/secsoc/information-resources/publications-and-tools/policy-papers/WCMS_305947/lang--en/index.htm

UNDP/ILO/Global South-South Development Academy. 2011. Successful social protection floor experiences: Sharing innovative experiences, Vol. 18 (New York). Available at: www.ilo.org/secsoc/information-resources/publications-and-tools/books-and-reports/WCMS_SECSOC_20840/lang--en/index.htm.

Vargas, I. et al. 2010. "Barriers of access to care in a managed competition model: Lessons from Colombia", in BMC Health Services Research, Vol.10 No. 297, pp. 1-12. Available at: www.biomedcentral.com/1472-6963/10/297.

8

Lesotho: Old Age Pension[12]

The Old Age Pension (OAP) is a tax-based scheme for all older persons. This non-contributory social pension also benefits other household members, particularly children.

With more than 4 per cent of its population above the age of 70, Lesotho has a larger share of older people than many countries in sub-Saharan Africa. All citizens of Lesotho over 70 years of age are entitled to a monthly pension benefit of 550 Lesotho Maloti (LSL), equivalent to US$40. The OAP was introduced to lift older persons out of poverty and is the largest regular cash transfer in Lesotho, covering about 83,000 persons (4.5 per cent of the population). While coverage of eligible persons is approximately 100 per cent, it is estimated that many more benefit indirectly.

Prior to the OAP's introduction, only war veterans and civil servants received a pension, covering less than 3 per cent of older persons in Lesotho.

1. Main lessons learned

- The high prevalence of HIV/AIDS in Lesotho often leads older persons to become the main caregivers for their orphaned grandchildren. In such cases, the Old Age Pension also benefits children.

---

[12] This chapter was authored by Thea Westphal of the ILO and reviewed by Lucilla Maria Bruni and Ana Ocampo of the World Bank, and Isabel Ortiz, Valérie Schmitt, Betina Ramirez-Lopez, James Canonge and Loveleen De of the ILO. It was first published in March 2016.

- Lesotho's implementation of the Old Age Pension shows that high coverage is possible even in difficult geographic conditions.
- The OAP has always been fully funded and administered by the Government, which is proof that even a country with limited financial resources can afford a universal programme.
- Regular adjustments in benefit amounts indicate the continued commitment from the Government.
- The OAP in Lesotho demonstrates that in the initial years, the administration of a non-contributory pension scheme can be done manually.
- Lesotho's OAP experience shows that a universal social protection scheme which has high coverage can help garner political support among people and can be a key factor in the re-election of a government.

2. Why is the OAP needed?

Lesotho's share of elderly people is larger than in other sub-Saharan African countries. This can mainly be attributed to outmigration of young people and decreased longevity due to HIV/AIDS. The HIV/AIDS prevalence rate is 23.4 per cent and has significantly reshaped the country's demographics. Life expectancy is only 48 years and an estimated 360,000 children have lost either one or both parents to the HIV epidemic. Often, older Basotho become the primary caretakers of their grandchildren. In rural areas, 8 per cent of households are skip-generation households.

Furthermore, the incidence of poverty is high with 56.2 per cent of 1.9 million Basotho living on less than $1.25 a day. Households with people above 59 years of age experience higher food poverty than the general population (39.3 per cent compared to 34.2 per cent).

Against this backdrop, the Government of Lesotho introduced the OAP in 2004 to provide a basic income guarantee for older persons with the ultimate objective of lifting them out of poverty. In doing so, Lesotho became a pioneer in the provision of universal benefits for older citizens in sub-Saharan Africa.

From the beginning, the OAP has been an entirely national effort. The main drivers behind the OAP are the political will and commitment of the Government. The OAP played a significant role in the election outcome in 2007. In post-election surveys, voters indicated that the introduction of the old-age pension was a strong motivation to vote for the then governing party.

3. How is the OAP implemented?

Upon registration, pensioners receive a monthly payment of LSL550 ($40). The amount is announced in the annual budget by the Ministry of Finance.

At the outset of the OAP, a village-by-village registration and sensitization of communities was carried out by the District Administration, traditional village chiefs, and Members of Parliament. Following this initial registration process, new applicants now have to submit completed application forms at local government offices.

Payment process: Application forms are available at local government offices. Applicants must provide official proof of identity (national identity card, passport, or voter card). Applications are then sent to the Registration Section in the Pensions Directorate in the Ministry of Finance. The Registration Section approves the applications and enters the details of successful applicants into the payroll on a monthly basis.

The Pensions Unit in the same Directorate transfers funds to 300 payment points across the country on a monthly basis. These funds are physically carried by the army to the payment points. Successful applicants are paid monthly at their preferred payment point. They are identified and verified based on their identity card and signature or thumbprint. Payment points are mostly located in buildings of the national post.

Figure 11: Overview of the institutional set-up of Lesotho's OAP scheme

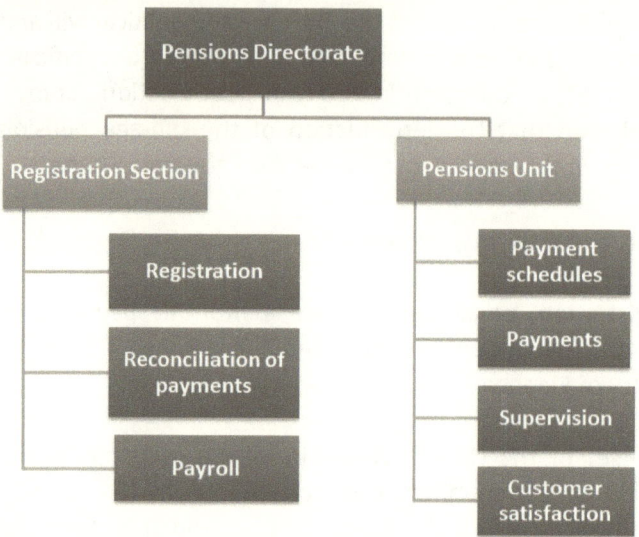

On a few occasions, remote payment points were served by helicopter because of weak road infrastructure. The national army provides security at service points and while transferring the money.

Random checks of payment points are conducted on a regular basis to ensure beneficiary satisfaction with service delivery. Due to the rudimentary information system, the systematic identification of ghost pensioners has so far been a challenge. It is suspected that the OAP is given to many ghost pensioners who are often created by under-reporting deaths of beneficiaries.

Reconciliation of payments is done manually against the payroll. Because this process is cumbersome there are some doubts as to whether it takes place systematically at the end of each month.

The management system for the OAP is manual. Beneficiary data and application forms are stored on paper only and the process is not well-coordinated. Currently, there is no regular monitoring and evaluation being done.

Financing: The OAP is financed by general taxation, which largely comes from revenues of the Southern African Customs Union. The total cost is about 1.7 per cent of GDP. Although OAP utilizes existing structures and government actors, the administrative costs are estimated to be quite high at around 20 per cent.

Complementary services and transfers provided as part of the national social protection system include subsidized or free primary health care at government health centres and government hospitals, free anti-retroviral treatment medication for HIV/AIDS patients, as well as a cash grant administered by local government for those deemed "needy" which OAP beneficiaries can receive too.

4. What is the OAP's impact on people?

The OAP not only benefits older persons, but also their grandchildren in numerous skip-generation households. Studies estimate that beneficiaries spend as much as 20 per cent of the benefit amount on dependent and orphaned children.

A large portion of the pension is spent on food, which has had a positive effect on food security. The number of beneficiaries who say they rarely or never had enough food declined from 20 per cent to 10 per cent after the introduction of the OAP.

Beneficiaries also reported spending on heating material, clothes, and education-related costs, such as school uniforms, shoes, and books (Thulo and Croome, 2006). Beneficiaries are also able to make purchases on credit from local merchants using future OAP payments as guarantees.

Finally, the OAP has contributed to empowering older persons by improving their financial status in the household and giving them a feeling of dignity (Wahenga, 2007).

5. What's next?

Lesotho has made considerable progress in building its national SPF. However, there is room for improvement.
- The eligibility age for the OAP should be lowered.
- Regular auditing of the OAP would be instrumental in identifying and removing ghost pensioners from the list of eligible beneficiaries.
- Coordination between implementing agencies could be improved, such as between the Ministry of Social Development and the Pensions Directorate. Improved coordination could also facilitate case management and referral of OAP beneficiaries to other government services. This could be done by initiating a social protection coordination committee.
- All OAP beneficiaries could in the future be included in the National Information System for Social Assistance (NISSA) in order to improve the application, verification, and payment processes.

6. References

Beales, S. 2007. How older people spend their pensions – Universal benefits: Delivering rights and reducing poverty, PowerPoint presentation, Feb. 2 (Help Age International).

Bureau of Statistics (Lesotho). 2013. Lesotho Demographic Survey, 2011 (Maseru).

—. 2008. 2008 Integrated Labor Force Survey (Maseru).

Cohen, B.; Menken, J. (eds.). 2006. Aging in sub-Saharan Africa: Recommendations for furthering research (Washington, DC, The National Academies Press).

Giovannetti, G. 2011. Social protection for inclusive development. A new perspective in EU cooperation with Africa, Robert Schuman presentation, Nairobi, 10 March.

Government of Lesotho. 2014. National Policy on Social Development (Maseru).

—. 2014. National Social Protection Strategy (Maseru).

Monchuk, V. 2013. Reducing poverty and investing in people: The new role of safety nets in Africa (Washington, DC, World Bank).

Olivier, M.; Andrianarison, F.; McLaughlin, M. 2013. Study on social protection in sub-Saharan Africa, Report (European Commission).

Oxford Poverty and Human Development Initiative. 2015. Lesotho Country Briefing (Oxford, University of Oxford). Available at: www.ophi.org.uk/multidimensional-poverty-index/mpi-country-briefings/.

Pelham, L. 2007. The politics behind the non-contributory old age social pensions in Lesotho, Namibia and South Africa, CPRC Working Paper 83 (Chronic Poverty Research Centre).

Smith, W.J.; Mistiaen, E.; Guven, M.; Morojele, M. 2013. A safety net to end extreme poverty, Africa Social Safety Net and Social Protection Assessment Series, Social Protection And Labor Discussion Paper No. 1409 (Washington, DC, World Bank).

Thulo, T.; Croome, D. 2006. Furthering national action to realise commitments to social transfers in Africa, paper presentation, Lisbon, 4 Oct.

Wahenga. 2007. Old Age Pension, Lesotho, Reba Case Study Brief Number 3 (Johannesburg, Regional Hunger and Vulnerability Program).

World Bank. 2014. Lesotho: Systematic country diagnostic (Washington, DC).

World Food Programme. 2015. Lesotho: Current issues and what the World Food Programme is doing. Available at: www.wfp.org/countries/Lesotho.

9

Mongolia: Child money programme[13]

Mongolia's universal Child Money Programme (CMP) is one of the country's flagship programmes and is an essential part of its social protection system, which is among the most progressive and comprehensive in Asia. In May 2015, the Government of Mongolia, together with United Nations (UN) agencies, agreed on recommendations to complete the social protection floor, thereby addressing remaining social protection deficits.

Among the recommendations concerning the social protection floor, stakeholders emphasized the importance of maintaining the universality of the Child Money Programme. Reinforcing the Child Money Programme's legal framework and adequacy of benefits is seen as the most effective response to tackle poverty, in particular rural poverty.

---

[13] This chapter was authored by Celine Peyron Bista and Lkhagvademberel Amgalan of the ILO and Enkhnasan Nasan-Ulzii of UNICEF, and reviewed by Gaspar Fajith, Roberto Benes and Catalina Gomez of UNICEF and Franziska Gassmann of the Maastricht Graduate School of Governance. It was first published in September 2016.

Figure 12: Definition of a social protection floor for Mongolia, formulated by the national dialogue in 2013-14

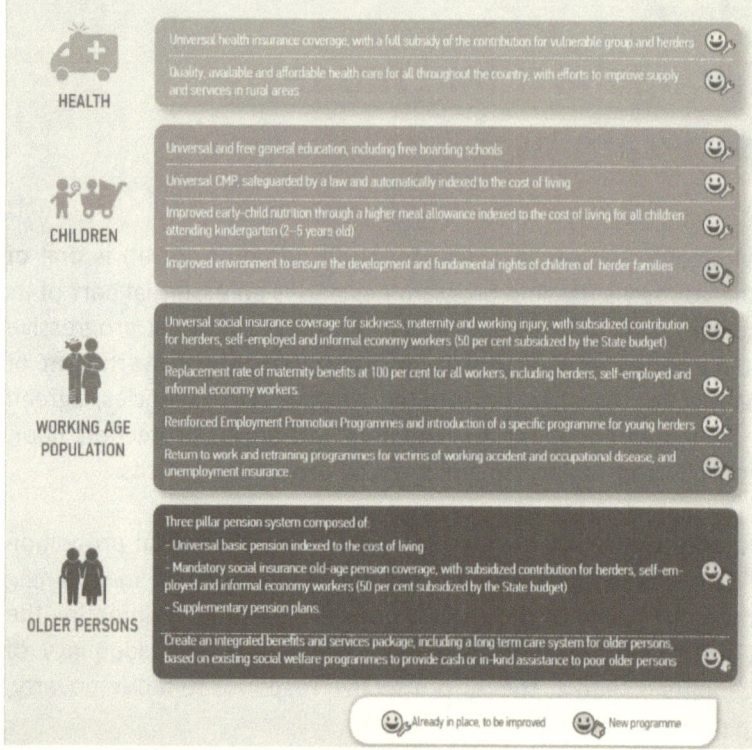

Source: UN and Government of Mongolia, 2015.

1. Recommendations for improving the Child Money Programme[14]

- The CMP has to be embedded in a legislative framework to safeguard its sustainability, coverage and adequacy.
- The programme should introduce an automatic indexation on the cost of living to guarantee its efficiency in terms of poverty reduction impact.

---

[14] These recommendations represent a consensus among stakeholders on the definition of an SPF for Mongolia, reached during the national dialogue conducted in 2013-14.

- Mongolia, being a middle-income country, needs to maintain the universality of its social protection while concurrently promoting decent employment and increased participation in its social insurance system in order to fully activate the redistribution function of the social protection system that goes beyond solely poverty reduction.

2. What does Mongolia's Child Money Programme look like?

Programme characteristics and reach: The programme, which went through different phases of development (see below) offers an allowance of 20,000 Mongolian tughriks (MNT) (around US$10 in June 2016) per month to all children aged 0 to 17 years old, including children in correctional facilities and those living abroad. However, children of migrant workers are not covered by the programme, a gap that was brought to the attention of the Government (ILO, 2016a).

The CMP is financed through the Human Development Fund (HDF), which is accumulated from mineral resource taxes. The CMP is perceived as a mechanism for redistributing wealth from the mining sector across the population in an equitable and efficient manner.

Two parameters of the programme can explain its success. First, the programme is **focused on children.** The main beneficiaries of the programme are children, which are automatically eligible at the time of civil registration with the State Registration General Office (SRGO) (no additional procedure is required). Second, the programme has an **effective payment mechanism**. The monthly benefit is paid directly through an automatic bank transfer to eligible families. As a result, by the end of 2015, almost 1.03 million, or nearly 100 per cent of children aged 0 to 17 years old, received this benefit (NSO, 2015).

Place of the CMP in the overall social protection system of Mongolia: The CMP is part of a comprehensive social protection system, reflecting the strong attachment of Mongolia's society to solidarity and social justice. This system has five main components: (a) universal social health insurance scheme that is partially or fully subsidized by the State for certain groups of the population; (b) compulsory and voluntary social insurance securing compensation and benefits in case of maternity, sickness, unemployment (only compulsory scheme), employment injury, old-age, disability and survivorship; (c) social assistance/welfare programmes financed from general tax revenues; (d) the Child Money Programme and other rights-based social protection allowances financed from mineral revenues through the Human Development Fund; and (e) active labour market policies, employment programmes and local development programmes (financed from the State's budget).[15]

As of the end of 2013, coverage under the mandatory social health insurance scheme was nearly universal, extending to more than 90 per cent of the population. In the same year, 71.6 per cent of the economically active population was insured under the social insurance system, either under the compulsory

---

[15] Mongolia provides an interesting example of a universal maternity benefit, as it offers universal maternity protection coverage through a combination of different mechanisms. Formal employees are covered by social insurance on a mandatory basis and receive a replacement rate of 100 per cent of their covered wages for four months. Herders, self-employed and workers in the informal economy can join the scheme on a voluntary basis and receive maternity cash benefits for four months at a replacement rate of 70 per cent of their selected reference wage after 12 months of contributions. In addition, maternity cash benefits under the Social Welfare Scheme are provided to all pregnant women and mothers of infants regardless their contribution to the social insurance scheme, status in employment and nationality. The benefit, equivalent to approximately $20 per month (2015) is paid from the fifth month of pregnancy for 12 months. Maternity care is provided through the universal (tax funded) health-care system (ILO, 2016a).

or voluntary scheme. However, those contributing to the voluntary scheme represented, in 2013, only 23.3 per cent of those who are eligible to participate, i.e. herders, self-employed, informal economy workers and the unemployed. The total coverage expanded to 85 per cent in 2015, a rise mainly attributable to increased registration among self-employed and herders under the voluntary scheme.

Figure 13: Overall structure of the social protection system in Mongolia

Source: Ministry of Labour and Social Protection, 2016.

In addition, the tax-funded social welfare system plays an important role in providing public support to members of vulnerable groups such as older people and people with disabilities, orphans, infants, women during maternity or single mothers with many children who are unable to live independently. Expenditures on 71 programmes stated by law targeting specific groups of the population accounted for 1.1 per cent of the gross domestic product (GDP) in 2014.[16] Social welfare expenditures more than doubled, increasing from MNT99.3 billion to MNT256.8 billion between 2010 and 2015,

---

[16] Source: Ministry of Finance, 1 June 2016. Programmes implemented by the Social Welfare Services General Office under the Law on Social Welfare, 2012; the Law on Social Security for People with Disabilities, 2005; Law on Social Security of Senior Citizens, 2005; and Law on Supplementary Allowance for Honored Senior Citizens, 2008.

resulting in 49.4 per cent of the population receiving some social welfare benefits, including the CMP allowance, and having a positive impact on poverty levels (Onishi and Chuluun, 2015). During the period 2010 to 2014, the national poverty headcount index decreased from 38.7 per cent to 21.6 per cent, and in rural areas from 49.0 per cent to 26.4 per cent (NSO, 2014).

Without the CMP, only 19 per cent of the population would receive social welfare benefits (Onishi and Chuluun, 2015). The CMP is therefore one of the flagship programmes of the Government, together with the universal Maternity Allowance paid over 12 months to all pregnant women, irrespectively of their activity and employment status.

As noted above, an important financing source of non-contributory social protection schemes is the Human Development Fund (HDF), established in accordance with the Law on Human Development Fund that was approved by the Parliament in November 2009. The HDF builds on revenues from the mineral and mining sectors and has an objective of redistributing wealth equally among all citizens of Mongolia. The Child Money Programme is one of the main programmes funded by the HDF.

In 2014, the aggregate expenditures for social welfare, state subsidies to the social insurance pension fund and social protection expenditures of the Human Development Fund amounted to 3.4 per cent of GDP.

3. Evolution of the Child Money Programme since 2005

Rising copper prices and swelling tax revenues resulted in a budget surplus in 2005, offering an enabling environment for strengthening social protection. In January 2005, the CMP was introduced as Mongolia's first programme targeting the poor. Households with three or more children and were identified as poor using a proxy-means test were entitled to an allowance if children had mandatory immunizations, lived with parents and were not engaged in the worst forms of child labour. In addition, for those with children aged 8 to 17 years old, the transfer was also conditioned on school enrolment. By June 2005, the programme had reached all its targeted population, or 61 per cent of all children aged 0 to 17 years old.

In 2006, copper and gold prices, as well as government revenues, continued to climb. In July 2006, the CMP was transformed into a quasi-universal programme by discontinuing the use of the targeting mechanisms, but retaining a soft form of the conditionality on school enrolment. The benefit remained the same until the introduction of a quarterly cash transfer of MNT25,000 for all children in January 2007.

In 2007, UNICEF conducted an assessment of the CMP impact on poverty reduction. The analysis showed that the efficiency of income targeting was poor due to flaws in proxy means testing and implementation issues. The analysis concluded that the 'universal' programme had a slightly larger impact on poverty reduction than a targeted programme due mainly to exclusion errors associated with proxy means testing.

In January 2010, the Government discontinued the CMP and replaced it by annual cash transfer of MNT120,000 to all citizens.

In September 2012, the newly elected Government issued a resolution to re-introduce the CMP, providing a cash transfer of MNT20,000 per month to all children under 18 years, financed from the HDF. This resolution continues guiding the CMP's implementation. The resolution kept the CMP unconditional and universal with a simplified procedure for implementation. Citizens apply at any commercial bank and open up an account to receive their children's money; the banks do not charge any service fees as part of their Corporate Social Responsibility.

Table 6: Summary of Mongolia's Child Money Programme

Timeframe	Level of benefit	No. of children covered	Targeting and conditionality
1/1/2005–1/6/2005	MNT3,000 per month	350,000	• Households living in poverty identified using means testing • Households with 3 or more children • Vaccination • Not engaged in worst forms of child labour • Enrolled in school • Living with parents
1/6/2005–1/7 2006	MNT3,000 month	650,000	• Households living in poverty identified using means testing • Vaccination • Not engaged in worst forms of child labour • Enrolled in school • Living with parents
1/7/2006–1/1/2010	MNT3,000 per month	932,000	• Universal coverage conditioned to school enrolment • Living with parents
1/7/2007–1/1/2010	MNT25,000 per quarter	932,000	
Since 1/10/2012	MNT20,000 per month	967,900	• Universal coverage without any conditionality

Source: Ministry of Population Development and Social Protection, 2015.

4. What are the main impacts of the CMP?

While no comprehensive impact evaluation of the CMP has yet taken place, several research findings confirm the progressive nature of the programme. Not only is the benefit incidence nearly twice as high in the poorest quintile compared to the richest quintile (Gassmann et al., 2015), the allocation of the transfer is pro-poor, with 34 per cent received by the poorest group (Onishi and Chuluun, 2015). Based on an analysis of the 2014 Household Socio-Economic Survey, the CMP significantly reduced monetary poverty. Estimations indicate that the CMP contributed to a 12 per cent reduction in the poverty incidence and reduced the poverty gap by 21 per cent. If only children are considered, the achieved poverty reduction is slightly higher. The CMP appears particularly powerful in reducing poverty in the countryside and in the western parts and the highlands of Mongolia (Tserennadmid, forthcoming).

5. What's next?

The general elections held in June 2016 are a critical opportunity to ensure that social protection remains a priority for the new Government amidst the current serious economic downturn. In August, the newly elected Government announced a number of measures to reduce public expenditures, including re-introducing the income targeting of the Child Money Programme. The targeting will be done using an existing household database (created through proxy means testing of households for a smaller food stamp programme), which reduced coverage to 60 per cent of children.[17] The fiscal situation appears to leave little leeway for belt-tightening measures – at least for the short term.

---

[17] As of November 2016, the CMP is paid in cash to 60 per cent of children with payments to the remaining 40 per cent of children deferred until 1 January 2019.

The debate therefore is expected to continue in Mongolia on how to find sustainable solutions for financing popular social protection measures, such as the CMP, and what forms of targeting could best sustain basic universal social protection. Advocacy for maintaining the universality of the Child Money Programme, as well as the social protection system in general, would require strong national evidence on programme impact and efficiency. The debate would also need to be informed by empirical evidence from other countries (including on sustainable ways of financing programmes). In this light, the possible ratification of the Social Security (Minimum Standards) Convention, 1952 (No. 102), would provide useful guarantees for sustaining Mongolia's social protection system, including the Child Money Programme.

6. References

Fajth, G.; Vinay, C. 2010. *Conditional cash transfers: A global perspective*, MDG Insights Issue Paper No. 1. Available at: www.unicef.org/socialpolicy/files/Conditional_Cash_Transfers_ A_Global_Perspective.pdf.

Gassmann, F.; François, D.; Zardo Trindade, L. 2015. *Improving labor market outcomes for poor and vulnerable groups in Mongolia*, 102320-MN (Washington, DC, World Bank).

ILO. 2016a. *Assessment of the social security legislation of Mongolia in view of a possible future ratification of the Social Security (Minimum Standards) Convention, 1952 (No. 102)* (Geneva). Available at: www.ilo.org/asia/whatwedo/publications/WCMS_462848/lang- -en/index.htm.

—. 2016b. *Financial assessment of the proposed reform to the social security system for older persons and a proposed new pension scheme for the herders and self-employed persons* (Ulaanbaatar). Available at:

www.ilo.org/asia/whatwedo/publications/WCMS_486332/lang--en/index.htm.

NSO Mongolia. 2014. *Report of the Household Socio-Economic Survey 2014* (Ulaanbaatar).

—. 2015. *Mongolian Statistical Yearbook 2015* (Ulaanbaatar).

Onishi, J.; Chuluun, T. 2015. *Review of program design and beneficiary profiles of social welfare programs in Mongolia* (Washington, DC, World Bank Group).

UNICEF. 2007. *Child benefits and poverty reduction: Evidence from Mongolia's child money programme* (New York).

—. 2015. *Cash transfer as a social protection intervention: Evidence from UNICEF evaluations 2010-2014* (New York). Available at:
www.unicef.org/evaluation/files/Social_Protection_Evaluation_Synthesis_Final.pdf.

UNICEF Mongolia. 2014. *Analysis of the situation of children in Mongolia* (Ulaanbaatar).

United Nations; Government of Mongolia. 2015. *Social protection assessment based national dialogue: Definition and cost of a social protection floor in Mongolia* (Ulaanbaatar). Available at:
www.ilo.org/asia/whatwedo/publications/WCMS_369999/lang--en/index.htm.

Tserennadmid, A. Forthcoming. *Analyses on effects of changes of CMP on income poverty of children through microsimulation of the Household Socio-Economic Survey data* (Ulaanbataar, UNICEF).

10

Rwanda: Progress towards universal health coverage[18]

The Government of Rwanda has made significant efforts to develop its health-care system at the national and community levels, making it possible for most people in the country to access affordable health care. This has helped to achieve near-universal health coverage and contributed to making ILO's Social Protection Floors Recommendation, 2012 (No. 202) a reality.

The social health protection system in Rwanda consists of Community-based Health Insurance (CBHI) schemes for formal and informal sector members, Rwandaise d'Assurance Maladie (RAMA), Military Medical Insurance (MMI), and private insurance schemes. While 96 per cent of people in Rwanda were covered by health insurance in 2011, CBHI had the highest coverage rate at 91 per cent. Started in 1999 as a pilot programme, it has since been rolled out nationwide. CBHI has greatly contributed to improving health standards in Rwanda, including increased life expectancy at birth and reduced child and maternal mortality.

1. Main lessons learned

- The experience of Rwanda shows that it is possible for low-income countries to meaningfully extend an SPF for

[18] This chapter was authored by Stefan Urban, Loveleen De and Hiroshi Yamabana with support from Victoire Umuhire and Cristina Lloret of the ILO and reviewed by Isabel Ortiz, Kelobang Kagisanyo, Anne Drouin, Théopiste Butare, Valérie Schmitt, Xenia Scheil-Adlung and Thorsten Behrendt of the ILO, and Kathy Kantengwa of The Global Fund. It was first published in April 2016.

health care and move towards universal health coverage, even when the vast majority of people live in rural areas and belong to the informal sector.

- Near universal coverage was achieved due to strong political commitment, a decentralized and strong network of health facilities in all districts, community participation, and the use of cultural elements like *Ubudehe* to include all people.[19]
- CBHI subsidizes contributions for the poor and vulnerable, which has helped to extend coverage to otherwise excluded groups.
- The linkages between health centres and hospitals and communities are strengthened by a total of 45,000 community health workers (CHWs).
- Simple technology can be used to conduct routine surveillance of health events and reach out to people in rural and remote areas.

2. What is Rwanda's social health protection system?

Over four years of civil war and genocide in Rwanda, close to 1 million lives were lost and the country was left in a state of near collapse in 1994. Since then, Rwanda has made striking achievements in rebuilding its health-care system and reaching near universal coverage. The following are the main health insurance schemes in Rwanda:

1. Rwandaise d'Assurance Maladie, which provides medical insurance to civil servants and employees of state-owned enterprises;
2. Military Medical Insurance, which provides basic insurance coverage to military personnel;
3. Community-based Health Insurance schemes, or Mutuelles de Santé, for formal and informal sector members; and
4. private insurance products.

---

[19] *Ubudehe* is the Rwandan practice of solving local problems through collective action and mutual support.

The Government of Rwanda's Vision 2020 and the Economic Development and Poverty Reduction Strategy provide for a health-care system that is based on health equity and developed using a people-centric, inclusive, and social cohesion-driven approach.

To extend coverage to all Rwandans, the Government launched CBHI as a pilot programme in 1999 with a nationwide roll-out in 2004. Coverage increased significantly from 7 per cent in 2003 to 91 per cent in 2011 and has helped promote the participation of communities in their socio-economic development.

3. What is the CBHI system?

Legal framework: The CBHI schemes are regulated by Law No. 62/2007 and statutory orders which contain provisions for their creation, management, and implementation, including the membership rules, package of services, provider payment options, and financing mechanisms. The Law states that every person in Rwanda not insured by any other health insurance scheme must join a CBHI scheme, thereby making affiliation to CBHI mandatory in nature.

Financing: The scheme is financed through various sources, such as member contributions, government subsidies, external donors, and other health insurance schemes such as RAMA and MMI, as seen in the Figure 14. Contributions are made on an annual basis and there is a waiting period of one month to access services. A co-payment is asked from members at the point of use of health services.

The contributions are based on a three-tiered premium scaling system called *Ubudehe*, established in 2010. *Ubudehe* assigns households into one of six categories, based on their income and assets. The premium of the two poorest and most vulnerable categories, i.e. 2,000 Rwandan francs (RWF), is fully subsidized by the Government. The two middle categories pay a slightly higher premium of RWF3,000, while the two highest categories pay the highest premium of RWF7,000. The National Income Categorization Database is used by local governments to classify the beneficiaries into one of six categories. *Ubudehe* introduced the principles of solidarity and inclusion in CBHI and contributed to improving its financial sustainability.

Figure 14: Funding sources for Rwanda's CBHI, 2012-13

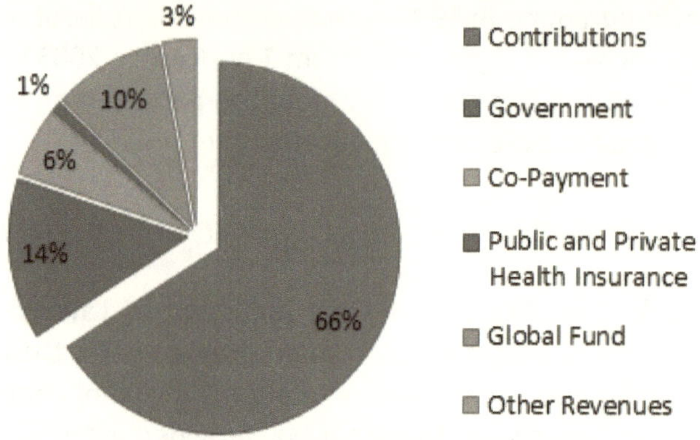

Source: Ministry of Health, Rwanda.

Implementation framework: Figure 15 shows the previous governance and financing structure of the overall CBHI system. In October 2015, the management of CBHI was transferred from the Ministry of Health to the Rwanda Social Security Board in order to improve the financial management and efficiency of the system. Figure 15 also depicts the decentralization of CBHI to the district and sector levels. [20]

Health-care services in Rwanda are delivered through a network of interconnected facilities. At the lowest level, health centres and health posts provide primary and preventive health-care services and offer pharmaceutical and basic laboratory support. District hospitals focus on preventive and curative services and health promotion. Provincial referral hospitals provide basic specialized services and have broader geographical coverage.

---

[20] Sectors are administrative subdivisions of a district.

National referral hospitals deliver specialized services and provide training tools and facilities for the expansion of medical services. CBHI members can access services at any of these facilities. The cost of ambulances is also covered.

Figure 15: Structure of the CBHI system in Rwanda[21]

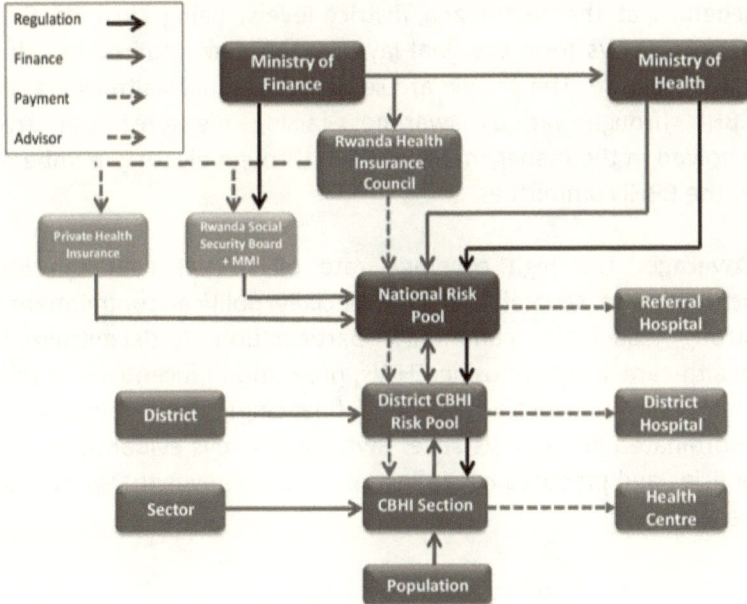

Source: Ministry of Health, 2010.

This system is complemented by a network of 45,000 community health workers who further contribute to strengthening the linkages between the health centres and hospitals and the communities. CHWs use simple mobile applications, such as RapidSMS and mUbuzima, to conduct routine surveillance and monitor health events. In this way, they facilitate case management and monitoring of health indicators.

---

[21] From October 2015, the management of CBHI was transferred to the Rwanda Social Security Board.

Furthermore, the Rwanda Health Management Information System, launched in February 2012, is a web-based application that is used to collect data from health facilities.

Decentralization and community participation are encouraged through management, implementation, and monitoring of CBHI schemes at the sector and district levels. Being close to the people, CHWs form the final layer in the decentralized health-care structure. The people are sensitized about health care and CBHI through various awareness-raising measures and are involved in the management of CBHI through electing members to the CBHI committees.

Coverage: The high coverage rate of 96 per cent can be attributed to several factors, especially political commitment, strong leadership, community participation, a decentralized health-care structure using CHWs, provision of incentives to the staff (i.e. performance-based financing), and effectively coordinated donor assistance. Rwanda employs evidence-based policies and practices by scaling up pilot initiatives that prove to be successful.

4. What are the key achievements in Rwanda?

The Rwandan genocide of 1994 and civil war had a devastating effect on the health-care system, creating a shortage of health workers and destroying infrastructure. Since then, the country has faced an enormous challenge to reconstruct its health-care system and infrastructure, improve the coverage and quality of health care, and tackle high HIV prevalence. This was done over a period of time through several measures, such as decentralizing services to the district level, installing the CBHI system, encouraging community participation in its management and financing, putting into place HIV and malaria programmes, and increasing immunization among children.

These measures have contributed significantly to improving health standards in the country. As seen in the Figure 16, life expectancy at birth for Rwandans fell sharply during the years of civil war and genocide. Since then, it has increased steadily to its current level of 64 years, which is higher than the life expectancy of 57 years for sub-Saharan Africa. The under-five mortality rate, which was among the highest in the world in the early 1990s, has declined to 42 per 1,000 thereby achieving the Millennium Development Goal (MDG) 4 on child health. Rwanda has also made significant improvements in reducing maternal mortality which stands at 29 deaths per 10,000 live births (World Bank, 2016).

Figure 16: Average life expectancy in Rwanda (in years)

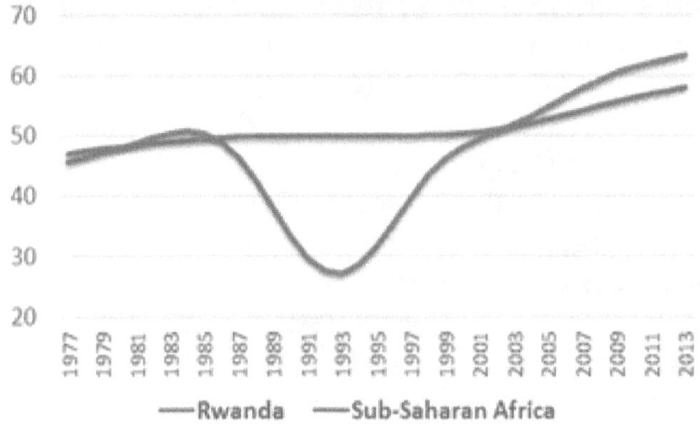

Source: World Bank, 2016.

CBHI has helped to reduce out-of-pocket (OOP) payments, as seen in Figure 17, making health care more affordable for its members. People can access care before their condition worsens, which decreases the total cost of treatment.

Improvement of infrastructure, especially in rural areas, has increased demand and access to health care and it is estimated that at least 60 per cent of the population lives within 5 kilometres of a health centre. Following the introduction of

CBHI, utilization of health care increased from 31 per cent in 2003 to 107 per cent in 2012.[22]

5. What are the challenges?

Declining enrolment rates: Even though health-care reforms in Rwanda helped to significantly increase coverage, there are still gaps in the implementation and universal coverage has not yet been reached. Furthermore, enrolment rates have declined slightly since 2011, partly due to incorrect categorization of members in the *Ubudehe* system. Some members are categorized as wealthier than they actually are and tend to drop out. Other members, whilst correctly classified, experience difficulties in paying the premiums due to seasonal or irregular incomes.

People also tend not to enrol unless they are in need of health care. This is facilitated by the fact that the waiting period of one month has not been strictly enforced. Furthermore, some members may access health-care services without paying the entire premium. There is no penalty system in place for such cases. Greater use of technology and mobile applications could help improve compliance.

Staff and financial deficits: According to Recommendation No. 202, universal health protection should be based on entitlements prescribed by law and constitute services that meet the criteria of availability, accessibility, and quality. Figure 17 shows five indicators to measure the deficits in effective access to health care in urban and rural Rwanda compared to Africa as a whole. While most Rwandan people were legally covered by health insurance in 2010, access to health services was still hampered for some 80 per cent of the population due to deficits in the professional health workforce and funds. The deficit in professional health workers such as doctors, nurses

---

[22] One person could utilize health services for different health problems.

and midwives was partly compensated by the large number of CHWs who visit people's houses to monitor health events and suggest early intervention. However, improvements are needed for effective and timely access to health care in Rwanda.

In addition to the insufficient number of skilled health workers, capacity building is needed for health workers and managers. Distribution of health workers across regions has to be made more equitable, especially between urban and rural areas.

Figure 17: Effective access to health care in Rwanda, 2010

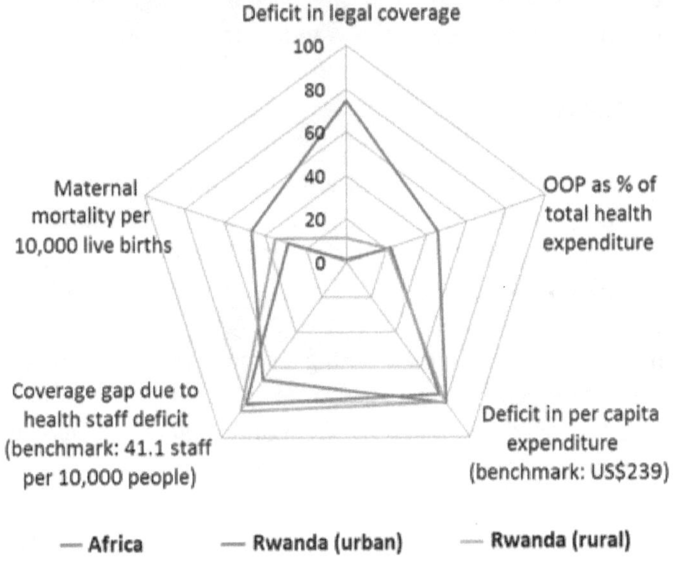

Source: Scheil-Adlung, 2015.

CBHI's low contribution rates have resulted in hospitals bearing large debts and patients having to buy drugs themselves from pharmacies without reimbursement. Further investments in the health-care system are needed at the national and district levels with an upward adjustment of contribution rates to help build financial robustness and sustainability. At the same time, the challenge of a large informal sector with limited capacity to pay their contributions on a regular basis and make their co-payments needs to be considered.

Next steps: Rwanda has made great advancements in providing health protection to its citizens through its focus on inclusion of the informal sector and people in rural areas. In this way, CBHI has supported the implementation of Rwanda's Economic Development and Poverty Reduction Strategy; however, more work is needed to address the current challenges in the health-care system. Some of these challenges, such as better financial management, greater efficiency, and better provision of quality health care, are envisaged to be addressed through the recent transfer of the operations to the Rwanda Social Security Board.

6. References

Binagwaho, A.; et al. 2014. "Rwanda 20 years on: Investing in life", in The Lancet, Vol. 384, pp. 371-375. Available at: www.thelancet.com/pdfs/journals/lancet/PIIS0140-6736(14)60574-2.pdf.

Habiyonizeye, Y. 2013. Implementing Community-Based Health Insurance schemes: Lessons from the case of Rwanda, unpublished master's thesis (Oslo, Oslo and Akershus University College of Applied Sciences).

ILO. 2014. World Social Protection Report 2014/2015 (Geneva).

Lagomarsino, G.; et al. 2012. "Universal Health Coverage 3: Moving towards universal health coverage", in The Lancet, Vol. 380, pp. 933-943. Available at: www.thelancet.com/pdfs/journals/lancet/PIIS0140-6736(12)61147-7.pdf.

Logie, D; Rowson, M.; Ndagije, F. 2008. "Innovations in Rwanda's health system: Looking to the future" in The Lancet, Vol. 372, pp. 256–261. Available at:

www.thelancet.com/pdfs/journals/lancet/PIIS0140-6736(08)60962-9.pdf.

Makaka, A.; Breen, S.; Binagwaho, A. 2014. Rwanda innovates to sustain universal health-care coverage (International Social Security Association (ISSA)). Available at: www.issa.int/-/rwanda-innovates-to-sustain-universal-health-care-coverage.

Ministry of Health. 2010. Rwanda Community Based Health Insurance Policy (Kigali). Available at: http://rbc.gov.rw/IMG/pdf/mutual_policy_document_final1.pdf

—. 2011. Service Packages for Health Facilities at different levels of service delivery (Kigali).

—. 2012. Annual Report: Community Based Health Insurance (Kigali). Available at: www.moh.gov.rw/fileadmin/templates/Docs/CBHI-Annual-Report-2011-2012f-3__1_.pdf.

—. 2013. Annual Report: November July 2012-June 2013 (Kigali). Available at: www.moh.gov.rw/fileadmin/templates/Press_release/MoH_Annual_Report_July_2012-June_2013.pdf.

Musango, L. 2013. "State of Health Financing in the African Region", in The African Health Monitor, No. 16, pp. 9-14. Available at: www.aho.afro.who.int/en/ahm/issue/16/reports/state-health-financing-african-region.

Nwaigwe, F.A. 2013. The mobile phone – Rwanda's key weapon in making maternal deaths history (UNICEF). Available at: www.unicefstories.org/the-mobile-phone-rwandas-key-weapon-in-making-maternal-deaths-history/.

Nyandekwe, M.; Nzayirambaho, M.; Kakoma, J.B. 2014. "Universal health coverage in Rwanda: Dream or reality", in Pan African Medical Journal, Vol. 23, pp. 1-8.

Rodríguez Pose, R.; Samuels, F. 2011. Progress on health in Rwanda: Leadership, performance and health insurance (London, ODI).

Scheil-Adlung, X. (ed.). 2015. Global evidence on inequities in rural health protection, ESS Document No. 47 (Geneva, ILO). Available at: www.social-protection.org/gimi/gess/RessourcePDF.action?ressource.ressourceId=51297.

World Bank. 2016. Life expectancy at birth, total (years). Available at: http://data.worldbank.org/indicator/SP.DYN.LE00.IN.

11

South Africa: Older Person's Grant[23]

South Africa is ranked as an upper-middle income country, but is characterized by high incidences of poverty and inequality. The Gini coefficient stands at 0.77 without considering the impact of the Older Person's Grant (OPG). Furthermore, inter-racial inequality is high with a mean per capita income in 2008 of 934 South African rands (ZAR) (US$76.9) and ZAR7,641 (US$614.3) for the black and white populations, respectively.

South Africa has a long history as a welfare state. Since the end of the apartheid era in 1994, the social protection system has played a crucial role in combatting poverty and inequality. It is also the first African country to introduce a social pension for older persons. The Older Person's Grant (OPG) is an income-tested grant provided to people above 60 years of age and varying between ZAR1,500 ($112) and ZAR1,520 ($114). It is estimated that the OPG along with other social grants brings down the high inequality in society from a Gini coefficient of 0.77 (without grants) to 0.60 (with grants) (OECD, 2015).

---

[23] This chapter was authored by Johan Strijdom and Oumar Diop of the African Union Commission, and Thea Westphal of the ILO and reviewed by Thomson Sithole and Anthony Makwiramiti of the South African Department of Social Development, and Isabel Ortiz, Valérie Schmitt and Loveleen De of the ILO. It was first published in August 2016.

1. Main lessons learned

- South Africa has demonstrated that extending social protection to older persons is feasible and affordable for middle-income countries.
- In particular, it is essential to have political will and commitment to increase public social protection expenditures. Today, South Africa redistributes roughly 3.5 per cent of its GDP through social assistance programmes.
- Along with other grants, the OPG is one of the most important tools for poverty reduction in the country. This is evidenced by the reduction in poverty incidence among older persons from 55.6 per cent in 2006 to 36.2 per cent in 2011.
- OPG also promotes gender equality (eligibility ages for males and females were harmonized in 2011) and addresses inter-racial disparity, through a gradual harmonization of the benefit amounts for different racial groups.
- The creation of a specialized institution, the South African Social Security Agency (SASSA), made delivery of social grants transparent and independent from political considerations.
- South Africa uses an integrated system for grant delivery and monitoring and evaluation (M&E). The integrated M&E system helps to continuously improve delivery. Biometric identification of beneficiaries limits the chances for identity theft.

2. How was the Older Person's Grant developed?

Means-tested social pensions were introduced in 1928. Originally, a social pension existed primarily for white male workers who had no access to occupational pensions and mixed-race women over 60 years of age. In 1982, trade unions were formed to represent and advocate the rights of African workers.

The unions succeeded in advocating the expansion of the Older Person's Grant to Africans. Furthermore, the amount of the grant was gradually harmonized for different racial groups with a view to achieve parity. During the 1980s, the pension for the black population was increasingly raised while that for the white minority was decreased. By 1992, the means test was equalized for everyone regardless of race, which led to an increase of the income threshold for the black population.

Figure 18: Maximum Older Person's Grant paid to South African black and white pensioners, 1925-2000

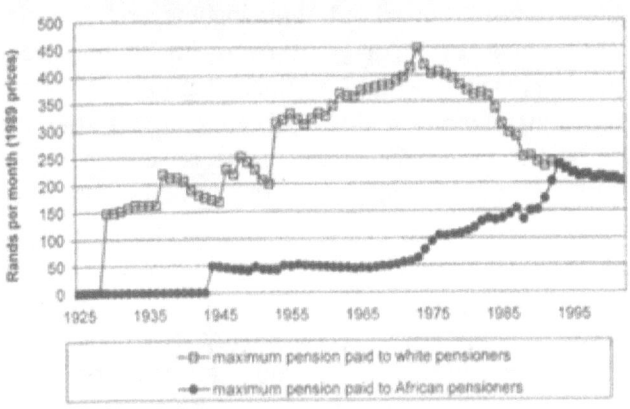

Source: Seekings/Nattrass 2005: 131

Source: Seekings and Nattrass, 2005, 131.

The design of South Africa's OPG has changed significantly in the last decade. Two of these design changes have significantly contributed to achieving social protection for all. Firstly, when it was introduced in 1928, it entitled all white men older than 65 years and mixed-race women over 60 years of age to an old-age grant. Over time, OPG was expanded to the rest of the population – including citizens, permanent residents and refugees with legal status – and the eligibility age for men and women was equalized to 60 years in 2011. Secondly, the grant is delivered based on criteria defined by the Department of Social Development (DSD) and applied by SASSA to ensure that decisions are transparent and replicable. The DSD is responsible for policy formulation and implementation support, while SASSA is an entity within the DSD that administers social grants.

3. What does the OPG look like?

Benefits and coverage: OPG is an income-tested, monthly payment of ZAR1,500 ($112) for persons aged 60-75 years and ZAR1,520 ($114) for those above 75 years. It is paid to around 3 million older persons in South Africa, reaching up to 100 per cent coverage in some jurisdictions. The OPG is given to citizens, permanent residents and refugees with legal status. Applicants have to provide information about their income and financial assets for the means test. If a grant needs to be reviewed, additional documentation is required, including greater details on the reported income and a life certificate to prove that the beneficiary is still alive. SASSA conducts the review and must notify beneficiaries three months prior to the review. In cases where payments are made electronically, the review automatically takes place once a year.

Geographic variation in coverage is mostly due to income differences between regions. The highest effective coverage rates are found in the metropolitan region of Johannesburg and Pretoria.

Operational arrangements: With the establishment of SASSA in 2006, delivery of the OPG has improved significantly as the scheme is now underpinned by coherent and transparent guidelines. Biometric identification is used at pay points to mitigate risks such as theft of the Personal Identification Number (PIN) and identity theft. At the time of enrolment, beneficiaries provide their photograph, fingerprints and voice recordings in English or seven vernacular languages. This information is saved in the database of the payment operator and a SASSA-branded MasterCard is given to each beneficiary, which serves as the identity and payment card. Voice verification is offered as an alternative to certify beneficiaries who use PIN code identification and at points where no fingerprint scanners are available.

SASSA contracts Cash Payment Services (CPS) to disburse the social grants nationwide. CPS works in partnership with Grindrod Bank, which issues bank cards to beneficiaries. The account is free of monthly charges and allows full access to traditional banking services, including ATMs, electronic fund transfers and point of sale transactions. SASSA cardholders can also transact offline where there is no formal banking infrastructure. Every channel requires beneficiaries to be identified through their SASSA card, which can only be done through successful biometric identification. Beneficiaries who use a PIN are identified through the PIN code and voice recordings. In this way, the payment remains secure and beneficiaries' identities can be verified even when there are no fingerprint scanners.

SASSA delivers benefits through fully equipped and well-staffed mobile units as part of its Integrated Community Registration Outreach Programme (ICROP). The ICROP facilitates beneficiary enrolment and registration, issues smart cards, maintains an online database, raises awareness, provides access to pay points and conducts home visits by medical staff and social workers to ensure that individuals unable to go to the hospital or leave their homes—due to disability or sickness—have access to services and benefits.

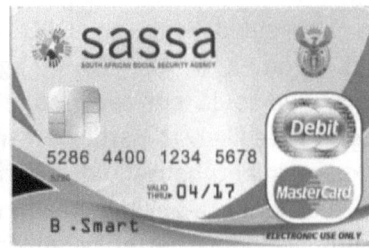

Mobile payment unit   SASSA-branded MasterCard

Payment channels: Three different payment channels exist, all of which use the SASSA card. The first channel is SASSA pay point areas, where the payment provider, CPS, sets up mobile ATMs. The second channel is payment into Grindrod bank accounts. The third channel is payment at institutions, such as old persons' homes on a fixed date, where beneficiaries must authenticate their identity with their SASSA card. Payment dates vary and are released a little in advance to prevent robberies of the trucks carrying cash. Armed security guards are present at pay point areas.

4. What are the main impacts on people's lives?

Recipients of the OPG share their pensions within the households. Estimates indicate that one grant reaches up to six persons in a recipient's household. Family structures in South Africa are fluid and often multi-generational rather than nuclear, which is largely due to segregation policies of the apartheid era and high HIV/AIDS prevalence. An HIV/AIDS prevalence rate of 18 per cent among the working age population leads to many people having chronic illnesses and disabilities. Older persons often raise their grandchildren because the parents may have passed away due to HIV/AIDS-related illnesses. In such circumstances, the grants serve as a reliable source of income and are shared within large households. Compared to non-recipient households, households that receive the OPG have higher shares of expenditures on food and education.

Research has shown that there is a positive correlation between living in a household with an OPG recipient and finding employment. Women in the 20-30 age group in recipient households are up to 15 per cent more likely to be employed and 9 per cent more likely to participate in the labour force than those in non-recipient households. Recipient households are more likely to experience positive health outcomes for children, especially girls, including better height-for-age and weight-for-height.

5. What's next?

South Africa has come a long way since the end of the apartheid era in 1994. Today, its social protection system is one of the most comprehensive in the region. While OPG is currently a means-tested benefit, DSD plans to universalize the grant. Different models have been financially assessed since 2013 and tripartite consultations with stakeholders and representative bodies have been carried out to choose the most suitable policy option. Universalization of OPG is a priority in South Africa because it is more accepted politically than universalization of other grants. Older persons still suffer from the long-term effects of apartheid and are often perceived as being needier than other groups.

South Africa is considering introducing a mandatory contributory social insurance scheme that provides pension, death and disability benefits. This will help to provide adequate and affordable benefits, pool risks across the labour force and achieve social solidarity, complementing both non-contributory social assistance and private insurance.

Another gap in South Africa's existing social protection system is the lack of income support for unemployed persons of working age, i.e. between 19 and 59 years old. This may result in the redistribution of OPG and other grants to unemployed members of beneficiary households, thereby lessening the impact on the intended beneficiaries and creating implicit subsidies for unemployed persons without a defined strategy or scheme to provide protection.

6. References

Finn, A.; Leibbrandt, M.; Woolard, I. 2009. Income & expenditure inequality: Analysis of the NIDS Wave 1 dataset, Discussion Paper No. 5 (Cape Town, University of Cape Town).

Government of South Africa. n.d. Department of Social Development, poverty and inequality data for 2014/2015.

—. 2015. Older Persons Grant. Available at: www.gov.za/services/social-benefits-retirement-and-old-age/old-age-pension.

Hagen-Zanker, J.; Morgan, J.; Meth, C. 2011. South Africa's cash social security grants: Progress in increasing coverage (London, Overseas Development Institute).

Interview with Thomson Sithole, Directorate Disability and Older Persons benefits, Department of Social Development. 2015. (Pretoria).

Leubolt, B. 2014. Social policies and redistribution in South Africa, Global Labour University Working Paper No. 25 (Geneva, International Labour Office; Global Labour University).

Noble, M.; Barnes, H.; Wright, G.; Noble, S. 2006. The Old Age Grant: A sub-provincial analysis of eligibility and take up in January 2004 (Pretoria, National Department of Social Development, Republic of South Africa).

OECD. 2015. OECD Economic Surveys: South Africa. Available at: www.treasury.gov.za/publications/other/OECD%20Economic%20Surveys%20South%20Africa%202015.pdf.

Oosthuizen, M. 2012. South Africa's state old age pension, presented at Recent Developments in the Role and Design of Social Protection Programmes Workshop, Brasilia, 3-5 Dec.

Seekings, J.; Nattrass, N. 2005. Class, Race, and Inequality in South Africa (Yale University Press).

Statistics South Africa. 2014. Statistical release P0211, Quarterly Labour Force Survey Quarter 4, 2014 (Pretoria).

12

South Africa: Disability grant[24]

According to its 2011 Census, 2.87 million people in South Africa, or 7.5 per cent of the population, lives with a disability. It is one of the only countries in sub-Saharan Africa to provide an allowance for people with disabilities (PWDs).

The South African National Development Plan 2010–30 emphasizes the need for an inclusive social protection system to address vulnerability and responds to the needs of persons with disabilities, older persons, children and particularly orphans.

The Disability Grant (DG) is provided to adults over 18 years of age and is the only non-contributory allowance provided to persons of working age in the country. The grant also covers persons with chronic illnesses such as HIV/AIDS, which has a prevalence of 18 per cent among people between the ages of 15 to 49 years.[25] The amount of the grant stands at 1,500 South African rands (ZAR) (US$112) and is fairly generous, considering South Africa's status as a middle-income country.

---

[24] This chapter was authored by Johan Strijdom and Oumar Diop of the African Union Commission, and Thea Westphal of the ILO and reviewed by Johanna Sekele of the South African Department of Social Development, and Isabel Ortiz, Valérie Schmitt and Loveleen De of the ILO. It was first published in August 2016.

[25] People with chronic illnesses benefit from the Disability Grant, but this is not legislated.

1. Main lessons learned

- South Africa has demonstrated that the extension of social protection to persons with disabilities is feasible and affordable for middle-income countries.
- Social grants for people with disabilities go beyond compensation for extra daily living costs caused by long-term ill health or disability. They provide an income replacement for those unable to engage in paid work and compensate for the loss of income for those who have a partial loss of earnings due to their disability.
- It is essential to have political will and commitment from the government, particularly to increase public expenditures on social protection. Today, South Africa redistributes roughly 3.5 per cent of its GDP through social assistance programmes.
- The creation of a specialized management institution, namely the South African Social Security Agency (SASSA), made delivery of grants transparent and independent from political considerations and the payment channels made it easier to reach people in difficult situations and remote areas.

Figure 19: Beneficiaries of South Africa's DG benefit, 1997-13

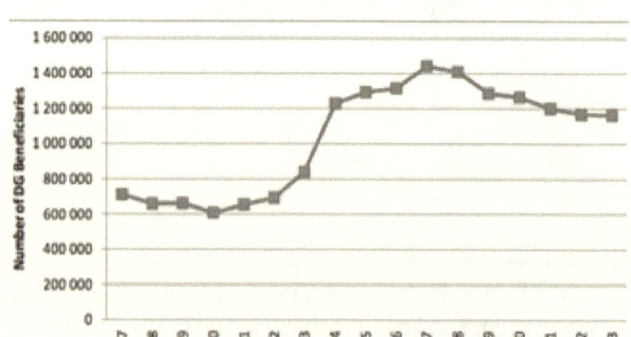

Source: Department of Welfare and DSD Annual Reports 1997-2013.

2. How did the Disability Grant develop?

The Disability Grant was one of the first social security schemes to be introduced as a means-tested benefit in 1937. It initially was targeted at the poor white population. In 1947, the DG was extended to all South Africans, but with different benefit levels and different income thresholds depending upon race. Incremental harmonization began in the 1970s and parity between races was reached only by way of the South African Social Assistance Act in 1992. Today, the DG covers nearly 1.2 million beneficiaries. It is paid to citizens, permanent residents and persons with "refugee status" in South Africa.

In South Africa, two institutions are active in the design and delivery of social protection. The Department for Social Development (DSD) is responsible for policy-making and oversight while the South African Social Security Agency, created in 2006, administers and delivers all social grants. The creation of SASSA reduced fragmentation and inconsistency within the previous system, where the benefit levels and eligibility criteria for social grants were decided by nine different regions and disbursed by different paymasters.

SASSA delivers benefits through fully equipped and well-staffed mobile units as part of its Integrated Community Registration Outreach Programme (ICROP). The ICROP facilitates beneficiary enrolment and registration, issues smartcards, maintains an online database, raises awareness, provides access to pay points, and conducts home visits by medical staff and social workers to ensure that individuals unable to go to the hospital or leave their homes—due to disability or sickness—have access to services and benefits.

In 2007, South Africa ratified and signed the UN Convention on the Rights of Persons with Disabilities (UNCRPD). The Convention facilitates the enforcement of the rights of persons with disabilities and requires states to take actions to improve PWDs' living conditions by providing support to help them to develop to their full capacities. Additional provisions are also contained in the Continental Plan of Action of the African Decade of Persons with Disabilities (2010-2019), the African Union policy instrument on disabilities.

Prevalence of HIV/AIDS in South Africa is 18 per cent among people between the ages of 15 and 49 years. Currently, a person living with HIV is eligible for the DG if it has resulted in some kind of activity limitation and if the CD4 count used to assess the immune system of a patient is below a certain threshold. For people living with HIV, the DG is the only non-contributory scheme that provides income security in case of loss of work capacity due to HIV infection and free health care. In 2003, 41 per cent of the DG beneficiaries were people suffering from "retroviral disease" or "immuno-compromised".

In 2004, the Government introduced free anti-retroviral drugs (ARVs), which significantly improved the health conditions of people living with HIV. Many of those who had significant improvements in CD4 counts lost their eligibility to the DG. This may explain why the number of DG beneficiaries has steadily declined since 2007 (see
Figure **19**).

3. What benefits are provided?

Persons living with a physical or mental disability which prevents them from working for more than six months can apply for a temporary or permanent DG. Their eligibility is determined through a medical assessment done by a doctor either from the Department of Health or contracted with SASSA.

Further eligibility criteria include an income-based means test and valid identity documents. The grant may be paid temporarily for between six and 12 months or permanently. The monthly amount of the grant is ZAR1,500 ($112) and lapses upon death of the beneficiary, failure to claim for three consecutive months, absence from South Africa or admission to a state institution for care. If the state institution has a contract with the State to care for beneficiaries of the DG, the DG is reduced to 25 per cent of the maximum amount for four months after admission to the institution. Upon discharge, the full DG is re-instated.

Eligibility for the grant is reassessed regularly for temporary Disability Grant payments. Coverage of the DG grew from 611,325 beneficiaries in 2000 to 1.24 million eligible persons in 2015. Complementary programmes for recipients include free health care and being allowed to apply for "indigent status" to support households to pay for water, electricity and accommodation. The Reconstruction and Development Programme (RDP) provides free retrofit houses with accessible features to any South African citizen with a disability and a monthly income of less than ZAR3,500 ($288).

Two additional grants are available to support DG beneficiaries. The Grant-in-Aid aims to support persons in need of support or care by another person because of their physical or mental disability. It is available for the beneficiaries of the DG, the Older Person's Grant and the War Veterans Grant. The Social Relief of Distress (SRD) programme serves as temporary assistance for applicants to overcome financial pressure during the application period (up to 21 days). Depending on how a disability has been acquired, beneficiaries may also be eligible for grants from the Road Accident Fund, the Unemployment Insurance Fund or Compensation for Occupational Injuries and Diseases Fund.

South Africa still struggles with strong social inequality with a GINI coefficient of 0.69 after social grants have been disbursed to beneficiaries.

4. What is the impact on people's lives?

In a society where unemployment stands at 24.3 per cent, many PWDs report being stigmatized and experience severe barriers to access the labour market. The DG provides some level of support to facilitate inclusion of PWDs in the labour market.

However, these protective measures need to be complemented by job creation strategies and campaigns to educate employers not to discriminate against persons with disabilities.

Research into the impact of the DG has so far been limited. According to available studies, 77 per cent of recipients cite food as their first item of expenditure and 59 per cent say that food is the item on which they spend most of their money. Recipients also spend money on electricity and water bills, which varies with the infrastructure available in the regions. Other expenditure items are purchases of clothes, funeral policies, debt repayments, rent payments, payment of school fees and remittances. Receipt of the DG, like all other grants, facilitates financial inclusion of recipients because all beneficiaries have an electronic smartcard for identification and payments. The DG benefits the households of persons with disabilities or living with HIV, and therefore has direct or indirect impacts on the livelihoods of a larger population.

5. What's next?

In future, links with employers and affirmative action policies to integrate persons with disabilities into the labour market should be pursued and prioritised to enable beneficiaries to graduate from poverty. This is already envisaged in the National Development Plan 2030 and required by the UNCRPD. To remove the barriers for PWDs, the policy framework for integration of PWDs exists and needs to be operationalized through pro-active and social understanding of disabilities.

6. References

De Paoli, M. M.; Mills, E.A; Grønningsæter, A.B. 2012. "The ARV roll out and the disability grant: a South African dilemma?", in Journal of the International AIDS Society, Vol.15, No. 6.

Interview with Thomson Sithole, Directorate Disability and Older Persons benefits, Department of Social Development. 2015. (Pretoria).

Johannsmeier, C. 2007. The social and economic effects of the Disability Grant for people with disabilities and their households – A qualitative study in KwaZulu Natal Province, Research Report No. 74. Available at:
https://opendocs.ids.ac.uk/opendocs/handle/123456789/1735.

Kelly, G. 2013. Regulating access to the disability grant in South Africa, 1990-2013, Centre for Social Science Research. Working Paper No. 330 (Cape Town, University of Cape Town).

Leubolt, B. 2014. Social policies and redistribution in South Africa, Global Labour University working paper: No. 25 (Geneva, International Labour Office; Global Labour University).

Mandonsela, V. 2010. South Africa's basic social protection floor, presentation at the Special Event on South-South Cooperation, United Nations HQ, New York.

Nattras, N. 2006. Disability and welfare in South Africa's era of unemployment and AIDS, CSSR Working Paper No. 147 (Cape Town).

SASSA. 2013. Implementation of CROP in South to enable the socially excluded and isolated access to Social Protection, presentation at the Technical Workshop on South-South exchange on integrating social policies and the delivery of social protection floors, Siem Reap, 29 May.

Statistics South Africa. 2014. Census 2011: Profile of persons with disabilities in South Africa (Pretoria).

Stats SA Library Cataloguing-in-Publication (CIP) Data

13

Thailand: Universal Health-care Coverage Scheme[26]

In less than two years, Thailand implemented a health protection scheme covering 76 per cent of its population (about 47 million people).

The successful launch of the Universal Health-care Coverage Scheme (UCS) in 2001 benefitted from the convergence of three factors: political commitment, civil society engagement and technical expertise. The UCS is a tax-financed scheme that provides free health care at the point of service. The benefit package is comprehensive and includes general medical care and rehabilitation services, high cost medical treatment, and emergency care.

The UCS covers the people previously served by a collection of piecemeal schemes and the people who were without health protection particularly in the informal sector, the latter being equal to 30 per cent of the population.

The scheme has increased access to health services and reduced the incidence of catastrophic health expenditures. While it is not dedicated to the poor, its universal nature has pro-poor impacts. For example, the UCS benefits the lowest income quintile of the population more than any other segment.

---

[26] This chapter was authored by Thibault van Langenhove and Lou Tessier of the ILO and reviewed by Isabel Ortiz, Nuno Cunha, Valérie Schmitt and Loveleen De of the ILO. It was first published in November 2016.

1. Main lessons learned

- Civil society can play an important role in extending social protection to all by raising awareness among the population and actively lobbying politicians.
- Strong political commitment is crucial for the extension of social protection to all; this was clearly set as a priority in Thailand.
- A universal scheme can comprise cost containment mechanisms to ensure its affordability and long-term financial sustainability.
- The application of the universality principle and an emphasis on equity can result in pro-poor impacts.
- The implementation of the first guarantee of the social protection floor in Thailand has helped to develop the health-care infrastructure and generated a positive macroeconomic impact.
- Embedding the scheme in national law has contributed to ensuring the sustainability of the scheme.

2. Political commitment, civil society engagement and technical expertise shaped the UCS

The right of every Thai citizen to access health care and the right of the poor to free health care are addressed in the country's 1997 and 2007 constitutions. However, despite the gradual extension of health coverage since the 1970s and several pro-poor social protection and health policies, at the turn of the millennium approximately 47 million Thai people, mostly informal sector workers in lower socio-economic groups, had no health insurance or access to free health care. Furthermore, in 2001, out-of-pocket payments accounted for one third of total health expenditures.

Since the late 1990s, a group of reformists in the Ministry of Public Health (MOPH) and the Health Systems Research Institute had been documenting health inequities and developing evidence-based policy options to tackle them. Due to this knowledge and active communication, in October 2000 a group of 11 Thai NGOs formed a united front and declared their intention to support universal coverage.

The political window of opportunity came during the 2001 national election. The campaign slogan of one of the contending parties, "30 baht treats all diseases", captured public attention. Following the election, the Government was eager to move quickly to consolidate public support. It put in place bold financing reforms to achieve universal health coverage within a year. The UCS was launched in six provinces in April 2001, in an additional 15 provinces by June 2001, and nationwide by April 2002.

The stated goal of the UCS is "to equally entitle all Thai citizens to quality health care according to their needs, regardless of their socioeconomic status". This goal is based on the universality principle: the UCS was conceived as a scheme for everybody, not one that targets the poor, vulnerable and disadvantaged.

3. **UCS covers 76 per cent of Thai people through a comprehensive benefit package**

The principle of the UCS is simple: it aims at covering the 76 per cent of the population not covered by other social health protection schemes, such as (a) the Social Security Scheme (SSS) for private sector employees, and (b) the Civil Servant Medical Benefit Scheme (CSMBS) for government employees and government retirees, as well as their spouses, dependants under 20 years old and parents.

Three features define the UCS:
- It is a tax-financed scheme providing free health care at the point of service (the initial co-payment of 30 baht per visit or admission was terminated in November 2006).

- It has a comprehensive benefit package with a focus on primary care.
- The budget is allocated based on a capitation payment mechanism for outpatient care and a global allocation based on diagnosis-related groups (DRGs) for inpatient care.

Figure 20: Coverage under social health protection schemes in Thailand, 2001-12

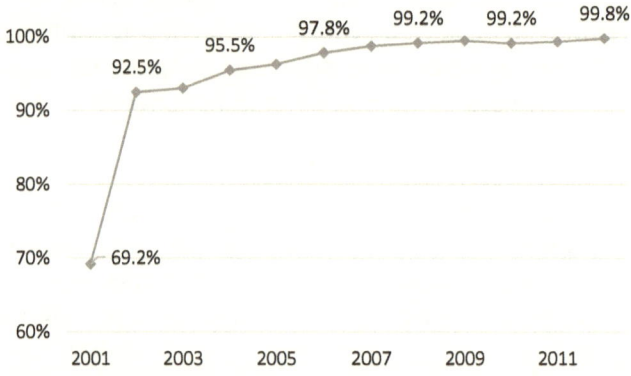

Source: National Health Security Office, 2013.

From the outset of the scheme, the package has been almost identical to that of the SSS, covering: outpatient, inpatient and accident and emergency services; dental and other high-cost care; and diagnostics, special investigations, medicines (at least including those in the National List of Essential Medicines) and medical supplies. The UCS also includes preventive and health-promotion services.

To control the cost and ensure the financial sustainability of the scheme, which requires more resources year on year, a fixed annual budget and a cap on provider payment were installed. The approved annual capitation rate tends to be lower than the amount requested by the health-care facilities, putting pressure on them to contain costs. Even so, the budget allocated to support the scheme has increased steadily every year. Although the total number of UCS members remained constant between

2002 and 2011 at around 47 million, the UCS budget rose from 1,202.4 baht per capita in 2002 to 2,693.5 baht per capita in 2011. This increase was mostly driven by increased utilization and rising labour and material costs of providing medical and health services.

The development of the UCS was done alongside a significant expansion and improvement of the health-care supply side, to ensure that health-care facilities could absorb the increased demand for services.

The UCS design called for radically different governance, organizational and management arrangements with a view to ensure more transparency, responsiveness and accountability. The National Health Security Act promulgated in November 2002 mandated the establishment of the National Health Security Office (NHSO) and its governing body, the National Health Security Board (NHSB), chaired by the Minister of Public Health.

The NHSO is responsible for the implementation of the UCS and hosts a common registry based on the Ministry of Interior's population database. This registry is shared with other social health protection organizations. Combined with the use of smart cards to identify entitlements at delivery points, this central database is crucial to ensuring the coverage of the entire population and preventing fraud. It has also allowed NHSO to produce data on the use of health services with a view to request an appropriate budget allocation and thereby better serve the population.

4. **Improved access to health care and contributions to economic growth**

There has been a gradual increase in the use of health services due to UCS. The number of outpatient visits rose from 2.45 in 2003 to 3.22 in 2010, and the number of hospital admissions per member rose from 0.094 in 2003 to 0.116 in 2010. Empirical evidence shows that this increase is particularly salient among poor segments of the population, particularly at health centres and district and provincial hospitals.

The share of catastrophic health expenditures (defined as out-of-pocket payments for health-care exceeding 10 per cent of total household consumption expenditure) dropped from 6.8 per cent in 1996 to 2.8 per cent in 2008 among UCS members in the poorest quintile, and from 6.1 per cent to 3.7 per cent among members in the richest quintile. Furthermore, an analysis conducted at national, regional and provincial levels concluded that there was a decreasing trend in health-impoverished households with one or more UCS members and that the degree of poverty reduction in this group was stronger than the overall trend in the same period.

Moreover, the UCS contributed significantly to the development of Thailand's health information system through hospital electronic discharge summaries for DRG reimbursement, accurate beneficiary datasets and data sharing.

Public expenditures on goods such as medicines and medical supplies have had spill over effects in various sectors, particularly chemical, trade, electricity and water, mining and quarrying, and transportation and communication.

5. Next steps

The NHSO's health expenditure projections until 2020 indicate that total health expenditure as a percentage of GDP will continue to increase, mainly due to the ageing of the population. To ensure the financial sustainability of the system, new measures will need to be explored. A long-term care system with an appropriate financing strategy also has to be developed to address the long-term care needs of people and avoid overburdening public hospitals.

Furthermore, there is a need to progressively harmonize the benefit packages and the provider payment mechanisms across UCS, SSS and CSMBS to reduce fragmentation, address equity issues and have greater cooperation, including a shared registry.

Finally, unequal distribution of health-care facilities between rural and urban areas and across regions affects people's access to health care. New incentives should be introduced to attract medical personnel, especially skilled ones, to rural areas to reduce the imbalances.

6. References

Health Insurance System Research Office. 2012. Thailand's Universal Coverage Scheme: Achievements and challenges. An independent assessment of the first 10 years (2001-2010) (Nonthaburi). Available at: www.jointlearningnetwork.org/uploads/files/resources/book01 8.pdf.

Hennicot, J.C.; Scholz, W.; Sakunphanit, T. 2012. Thailand health-care expenditure projection: 2006–2020. A research report (Nonthaburi, National Health Security Office).

Hughes, D.; Leethongdee, S. 2007. "Universal coverage in the land of smiles: Lessons from Thailand's 30 baht health reforms" in Health Affairs, Vol. 26, No. 4, pp. 999-1008.

Limwattananon, S.; Tangcharoensathien, V.; Prakongsai, P. 2007. "Catastrophic and poverty impacts of health payments: Results from national household surveys in Thailand", in Bulletin of the World Health Organization, Vol. 85, No. 8, pp. 600-606.

Nittayaramphong, S.; Pannarunothai, S.; Srithamrongsawat, S. 2000. Towards universal health insurance coverage (Nonthaburi, Health Care Reform Project, Ministry of Public Health).

Sakunphanit T. 2008. Universal health care coverage through pluralistic approaches: Experience from Thailand (Bangkok, ILO).

Schmitt, V.; Sakunphanit, T.; Prasitsiriphon, O. 2013. Social protection assessment based national dialogue: Towards a nationally defined social protection floor in Thailand (Bangkok, ILO).

Tangcharoensathien. V.; Swasdiworn, W.; Jongudomsuk, P.; Srithamrongswat, S.; Patcharanarumol, W.; Prakongsai, P; Thammathataree, J. 2010. Universal Coverage Scheme in Thailand: Equity outcomes and future agendas to meet challenges, World Health Report (2010), Background Paper, No. 43 (WHO). Available at:
www.who.int/healthsystems/topics/financing/healthreport/43ThaiFINAL.pdf.

Thai working group on National Health Accounts. 2011. National Health Accounts 1994 to 2008 (Bangkok, Ministry of Public Health).

14

Thailand: Universal social pension[27]

In 2009, Thailand succeeded in expanding pensions for older persons through the implementation of a non-contributory old-age allowance.

Until recently, Thailand's pension system included several contributory schemes for government officials, private sector employees and informal economy workers. However, coverage of the latter group was very limited. Overall, only 20 per cent of older persons had access to some level of protection.

In the face of an ageing population and a large informal sector, the country sought new ways to protect older persons without coverage. In 2009, a non-contributory old-age allowance was introduced and Thailand reached universal coverage soon afterwards.

1. Main lessons learned

   • In a country with a rapidly ageing population, a large informal sector and a relatively high incidence of poverty among older persons, a non-contributory pension can go a long way towards reaching those who do not have access to any social protection in old age.

---

[27] This chapter was authored by James Canonge and Loveleen De of the ILO and reviewed by Isabel Ortiz, Valérie Schmitt and Nuno Cunha of the ILO, Usa Khiewrord of HelpAge International, and Dr Thaworn Sakulphanit of the Health Insurance System Research Office in Thailand. It was first published in August 2016.

- Ineffective targeting procedures prevented needy as well as eligible older persons from receiving a pension. A universal scheme introduced in 2009 resulted in over 5.5 million new beneficiaries by 2013.
- Poverty among the elderly has fallen, which can largely be attributed to increased pension coverage. Increasing and indexing benefits, as well as strengthening the legal and financial foundations of the scheme, could further strengthen its positive impacts.
- Even though the benefit levels have increased steadily over time, the pension still does not provide sufficient protection. The non-contributory allowance can be complemented by additional schemes, such as the recently established National Savings Fund, which strives towards providing more comprehensive protection for people in old age. [28]

2. An ageing population with low pension coverage

While much of South-East Asia is characterized by relatively youthful populations, Thailand is ageing rapidly. Older persons will make up nearly one-third of the total population by 2050, as seen in Figure 21.

In 2020, the population of persons aged 60 and above is expected to surpass the number of children for the first time in Thailand's history.[29] Yet, until 2009, no more than 20 per cent received any form of old-age pension, often despite decades of hard work.

Thailand's pension system has continuously developed over the years and includes various schemes for government officials, private sector employees and informal economy workers. Depending on the number of years of contribution, government

---

[28] As the fund started in 2015, the effectiveness of the scheme cannot yet be assessed.
[29] Children are defined as persons below 15 years of age.

officials receive a lump-sum payment or a pension under the Pension for Civil Servants Act, 1951. Furthermore, they can also avail the Government Pension Fund, which provides a lump-sum payment upon retirement.

Figure 21: Population distribution by age group and sex in Thailand, 2010 and 2050

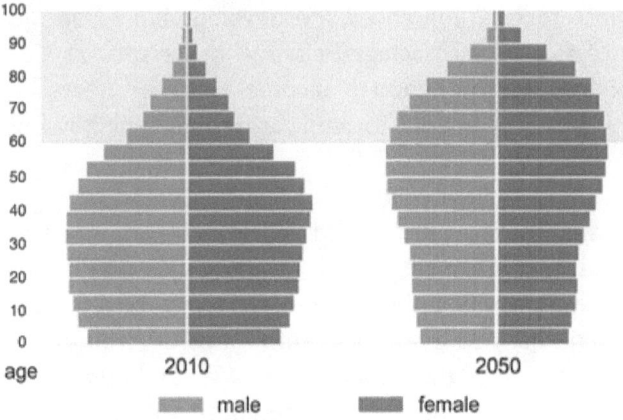

Source: UN Population Division (July 2012).

Depending on the duration of contributions, private sector employees can receive a monthly pension or a lump-sum payment under the Social Security Act, 1990 (section 33). Private sector employees can also contribute to a provident fund that gives a lump-sum payment upon retirement. Those who were previously insured under section 33 and cease their employment can continue to be insured under section 39. The contributions and benefits are based on a reference income of 4,800 Thai baht (THB), which is less than the minimum wage.

Workers in the informal economy can choose to contribute to one of two options under the Social Security Act, section 40. The first option does not provide any form of retirement benefits, while the second option provides a lump-sum old-age benefit. At the end of 2010, only 84 individuals were insured under section 40 (SSO, 2016).

3. A need for a non-contributory old-age allowance

Previously, there was a large gap in protection for informal sector workers. Even retirees from the formal sector lacked access to a pension because the contributory scheme was still young and the minimum number of years of contribution was not met. These factors influenced the development of an old-age allowance for "underprivileged elderly" or persons at least 60 years of age without enough income to meet necessary expenses, or who are unable to work, abandoned or have no caregivers.

The old-age allowance was designed at the national level, but was implemented through local authorities who were responsible for overseeing the scheme, selecting beneficiaries and paying benefits. However, local authorities differed widely in their interpretation of the national guidelines and application of the eligibility criteria. There was some abuse and leakages in addition to the exclusion of more than 50 per cent of the underprivileged elderly (Suwanrada and Dharmapriya, 2012, p. 158).

When it debuted in 1993, the allowance reached just 20,000 individuals. Reforms to the targeting methodology were made in 1995, 2002 and again in 2005, which resulted in increased representation of elderly advocates and local community members in the local committees in charge of the selection and disbursement processes. As a result of this and increased budget allocations, the number of beneficiaries went up steadily in the years that followed. Still, many eligible beneficiaries remained outside pension coverage. When the Government dropped ineffective targeting procedures altogether in 2009, coverage significantly increased.

Figure 22: Expansion of the old-age allowance in Thailand, 1995-2013

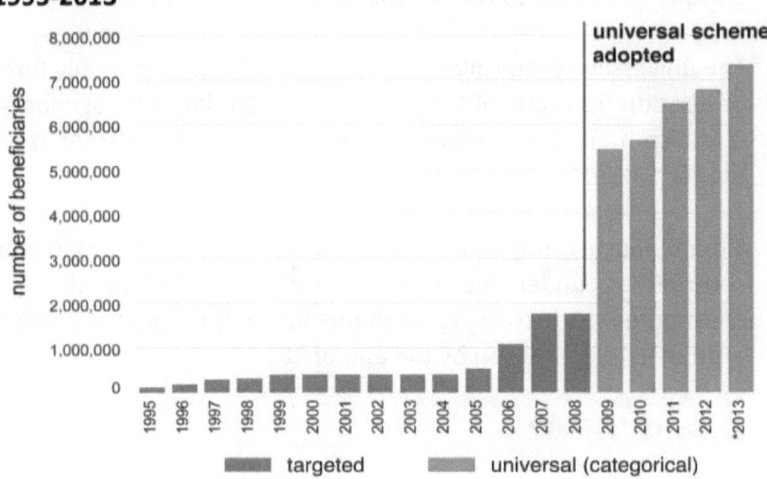

Source: ILO and UNDP, 2011.

4. A window for universal pensions

In April 2008, Thailand's government opted to implement the old-age allowance as a universal scheme as one part of its stimulus package to mitigate the global economic crisis and accelerate recovery. All individuals aged 60 and above residing outside of public elderly facilities and without access to regular pension payments became eligible for the benefit. As a result, coverage expanded remarkably.

Under the universal scheme, the supervision of the allowance is centralized under the Department of Social Development and Welfare with local bodies responsible for registering "residential inhabitants", a status required to receive the old-age allowance, and for distributing payments collected in person.

Registration happens once each year. Registrants can either appear in person at their local authority's office or sign up at a roving mobile registration unit. Payments are then either collected in person at the local authority's office or deposited directly into a bank account. Beneficiaries may also designate another individual to receive the benefits for them.

The universal old-age allowance serves as the first and only form of pension for many of those working in the informal economy. It is also a complementary source of income for retirees from the formal sector.

Simultaneously, the Government started to provide a matching contribution under the Social Security Act, section 40. This contributed to increasing membership of the voluntary social insurance to 2.4 million by the end of 2014.

5. What's next?

Since its introduction in 1993, the old-age allowance increased steadily from THB200 per month in 1993 to a maximum of THB1,000 in 2012, as seen in Figure 23. The adoption of a tiered methodology in 2012 recognizes greater need for income support as people grow older, due to the reduced capacity to work and increased health and long-term care needs.

Figure 23: Evolution of the old-age benefit in Thailand, 1993-2013

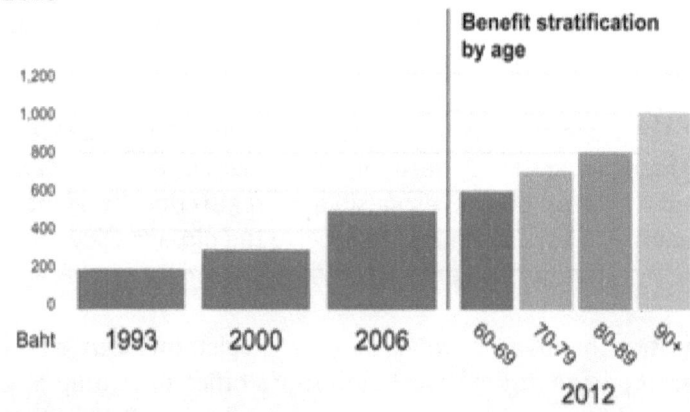

Source: ILO and UNDP, 2011.

While the extension of coverage and deepening of benefits has made discernible improvements in the lives of Thailand's older persons, the pension amount still remains far from the poverty line of THB2,647 per month in 2014 and minimum wage of THB300 per day. Indexation to the consumer price index, a percentage of the minimum wage or other benchmark could help ensure that the scheme provides sufficient income security for older persons.

In 2009, Thailand amended its Elderly Act to include the universal old-age allowance in national legislation. However, stipulations for setting benefit levels exist only in ministerial decrees, leaving it vulnerable to fiscal and political pressures.

For around 30 million informal economy workers who are not members of the Government Pension Fund or SSO pension scheme, the Government aims to reduce the income parity gap through the National Savings Fund, which started operations in 2015. Workers can contribute THB50-13,200 per year to receive a monthly pension of up to THB7,000 upon retirement.

6. References

Foundation of Thai Gerontology Research and Development Institute. 2015. National Old Age Pension System Reform (Bangkok).

ILO. 2009. Thailand. Pension reform in times of crisis: A report requested by the Ministry of Finance (Geneva).

Royal Thai Ministry of Social Development and Human Security. 2010. Amendment of the 2003 Elderly Act: The Act on Older Persons B.E.2546 (2003A.D.) (Bangkok).

Sakunphanit, T.; Suwanrada, W. 2011. "The 500 Baht Universal Pension Scheme – Thailand", in Sharing innovative experiences: Successful social protection floor experiences (New York, ILO and UNDP), pp. 401-415.

Schmitt, V.; Sakunphanit, T.; Prasitsiriphon, O. 2013. Social protection assessment based national dialogue: Towards a nationally defined social protection floor in Thailand (Bangkok, ILO).

Social Security Office (SSO). 2016. Social Security Fund: Number of Insured Persons (Article 40): 2007-2016 (Bangkok).

Suwanrada, W.; Dharmapriya, W. 2012. "Development of the old-age allowance system in Thailand: Challenges and policy implications", in S.W. Handayani and B. Babajanian (eds): Social protection for older persons: Social pension in Asia. (Manila, Asian Development Bank), pp. 153-167.

Wiener, M. 2012. "Thailand's matching defined contribution programs for the informal sector", in R. Hinz et al. (eds): Matching contributions for pensions: A review of international experience (Washington, DC, World Bank), pp. 275-286.

World Bank. 2012. Reducing elderly poverty in Thailand: The role of Thailand's pension and social assistance systems (Washington, DC).

15

Timor-Leste: Universal old-age and disability pension[30]

Despite being one of the youngest and poorest countries of the region, Timor-Leste has offered a universal social pension to its senior citizens and persons with disabilities since 2008. Almost all persons above 60 years and about one in five persons with disabilities participate in the scheme. The pensions support the well-being of beneficiaries and contribute to reducing overall poverty.

Timor-Leste's old-age and disability pension, SAII, was the first scheme targeted at older persons and people with disabilities to be introduced after the country gained independence. All citizens above 60 years and all persons with disabilities above 18 years are entitled benefits of US$30 per month. In its first year, the Programme covered more than 80 per cent of older persons, and by 2016, the Programme covered 94,287 individuals.

The Programme was introduced as one of the measures to improve social peace after violent conflicts in 2006. It remains the only old-age and disability pension scheme for non-public servants.

1. Main lessons learned

- The experience of SAII demonstrates that universal coverage is achievable in a short period of time, even in

---

[30] This chapter was authored by André F. Bongestabs of the ILO and reviewed by Isabel Ortiz, Valérie Schmitt, Nuno Cunha and Loveleen De of the ILO. It was first published in October 2016.

- countries with little to no infrastructure and in the aftermath of conflicts.
- Universal pensions can act as a social stabilizer in conflict situations. The introduction of SAII, together with other social provisions, is seen as an important element in the prevention of further social unrest in Timor-Leste after 2007.
- In societies with a large number of persons living in each household, such as in Timor-Leste, this type of pension scheme can have significant impacts on the well-being of the whole family and has the potential for positive intergenerational impacts.
- SAII has always been funded by the general government budget. This demonstrates that universal social pensions are affordable even for countries with fragile economies and limited financial resources.

2. What does the system look like?

Timor-Leste is a young country, where a large share of the population lives in poverty and most are vulnerable. In the aftermath of the 2006 East Timorese crisis, the Government of Timor-Leste put in place a set of cash transfer schemes, aiming to avoid future tensions and attend to the needs of the most vulnerable.[31] The first of these schemes was the Pension for Older Persons and People with Disabilities (Subsídio de Apoio a Idosos e Inválidos (SAII)), a universal pension for persons with disabilities and for those above the age of 60.

In a short time, other programmes were created, including benefits for veterans of the independence struggle and Bolsa da Mãe, a cash transfer designed for poor female-headed households with children. In 2012, the Transitory Social Security

---

[31] The 2006 East Timorese crisis was marked by riots and violence across the country as citizens took to the streets in their frustration with the apparent failure of the Government to deliver the advances promised at the time of independence in 2002.

Scheme, a non-contributory old-age pension for public servants, was created as a temporary programme. A contributory social security scheme is expected to start operating for both the public and private sectors in 2017. Free health care and education have been provided to all citizens since its independence in 2002.

Despite the progress made since independence, poverty is widespread and people experience reduced labour productivity and capacity as they get older. In a country where around 70 per cent of the population lives in rural areas and many people are engaged in production of their own food, older persons who represent around 6 per cent of the population, and people with disabilities were chosen as priority groups given their vulnerable status. Before the establishment of SAII, older persons and people with disabilities had to continue working or depend on their families for subsistence, as no programme provided support to this group after independence.[32] The first SAII payment was made in August 2008 and the scheme achieved substantial coverage among the elderly in its first year.

Coverage: Being a universal programme, all Timorese above the age of 60, or individuals above 18 who have a disability, are eligible for SAII. It currently delivers benefits to 94,287 individuals, which includes 86,974 older persons or 103 per cent of the target group and 7,313 people with disabilities or 18.2 per cent of the target group.[33] Individuals living abroad are not eligible and beneficiaries must have been living in the country for at least one year prior to receiving benefits.

---

[32] Before independence, they were part of the Indonesian system. After independence, contributions made to the previous system were lost.

[33] The coverage exceeds 100 per cent due to some inclusion errors or due to underestimation of the number of people above the age of 60 by projections based on the 2010 Census.

Figure 24 shows the evolution of coverage of SAII through the years. Public servants do not receive the SAII but are covered by a higher benefit provided by the Transitory Social Security Scheme, which pays old-age pensions calculated based on the average lifelong income of the beneficiary. Currently, this programme covers 688 former public servants.

Figure 24: Number of beneficiaries of the universal old-age and disability pension in Timor-Leste, 2008-15

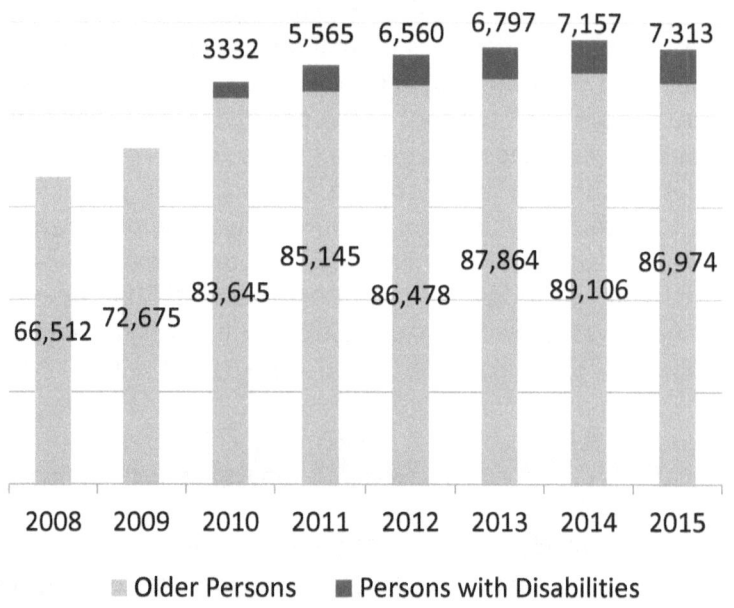

Source: Ministry of Social Solidarity.

Benefits: The benefit amount is the same for all beneficiaries. Its value is defined by official decree and it is limited to one third of the minimum wage of civil servants. When launched in 2008, the SAII benefit was $20 per month. The benefit was increased to its current value of $30 per month in 2010. The benefit is above the national poverty line but below the international poverty line. It stands at 7.9 per cent of the average household income in the country (see Figure 25).

Figure 25: SAII benefits ($360 per year) as share of various income indicators in Timor-Leste[34]

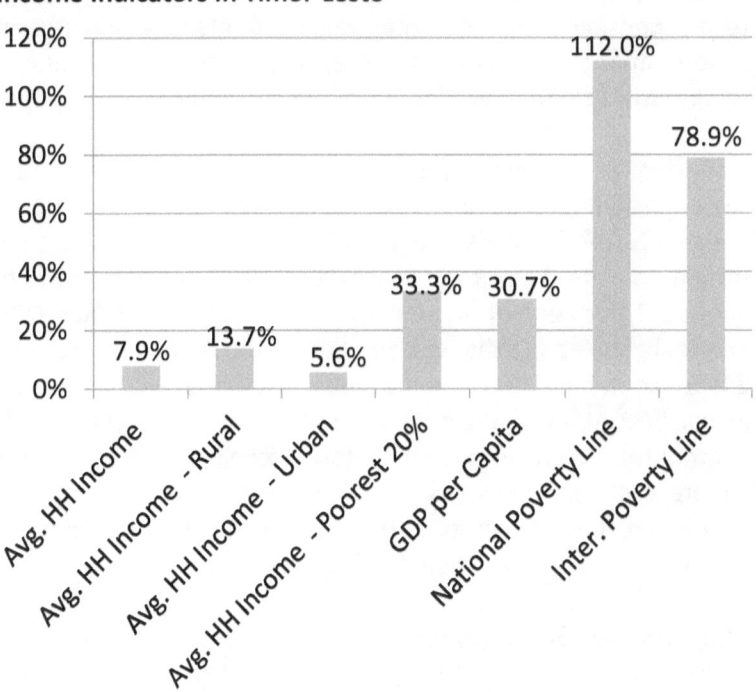

Source: HIES 2011; World Bank Database; Ministry of Social Solidarity; and author's calculations.

By law, benefits should be paid monthly by bank transfer or every three months in cases where payments are made directly. In practice, the lack of financial infrastructure, the difficultly in accessing isolated communities and limited resources for payment operations has resulted in payments being made twice per year.

---

[34] Average household income = $4,532.76 (2011); average rural household income = $2,624.52 (2011); average urban household income = $6,379.20 (2011); average household income of the poorest 20 per cent = $1,080 (2011); GDP per capita - non-Oil (2014) = $1,169; national poverty line = $0.88 per capita per day; international poverty line = $1.25 per capita per day.

Individuals receiving veteran benefits or benefits from the Transitory Social Security Scheme for public workers are entitled to the pension with the higher value. Additionally, inmates in prison and individuals in government social institutions temporarily lose the benefits while they are in these institutions.

Financing: All current social protection programmes in Timor-Leste, including SAII, are financed by the General National Budget. Currently, SAII's budget of $30.6 million along with $1.3 million for the Transitory Social Security Scheme represents about 2.2 per cent of gross domestic product (GDP) (non-Oil). This is slightly above the Asia and the Pacific regional average of 2.0 per cent, but still below the global average of 3.3 per cent of global GDP. While the global and regional figures include both contributory and non-contributory schemes, the current Timorese old-age pensions are exclusively tax-funded. Looking only at tax-funded pensions, Timor-Leste will likely be found in the higher end of investment in older persons globally.

Legal aspects: Social protection is a right in article 56 of the Constitution of Timor-Leste, according to which, "every citizen is entitled to social assistance and security in accordance with the law". Articles 20 and 21 reinforce the right to protection for older persons and people with disabilities.

SAII was enacted in June 2008 by Law Decree No. 19/2008, which described, regulated and effectively created the Programme. In August 2010, the "Diploma Ministerial Conjunto/MSS/MF/2010" increased the value of the benefit.

Institutional arrangements: The Ministry of Social Solidarity (MSS) is responsible for the SAII through the National Directorate of Non-Contributory Social Security (DNSSNC). Registration to the programme is done in partnership with the district and sub-district administrations (under the Ministry of State Administration), and payments are organized in cooperation with the Ministry of Finance and the National Bank. Local leaders (*Suco* chiefs) play a significant role in the identification of the beneficiaries and are responsible for confirming that the each older person lives at the specified location.[35]

When the creation of the Contributory Social Security Scheme has been approved by the Parliament, an independent institution will be created to manage and operate the new system. Once this occurs, the responsibility for administering the Transitory Social Security Scheme and SAII is to be transferred to the newly created National Institute of Social Security.

3. How was this achieved?

As mentioned before, SAII was developed partly as a strategy to mitigate the risks of unrest and instability due to widespread poverty and vulnerabilities, and partly as means to alleviate poverty. However, the creation of the universal pension scheme is solidly based in the Constitution, which expresses the right to social assistance to all and recognizes the extra attention older persons and people with disabilities require. Additionally, social assistance has been seen as an important tool for social stability from the first National Development Plan (NDP) from 2002. Furthermore, the NDP also foresaw the provision of support for older citizens and persons with disabilities, recognizing the vulnerabilities facing them.

In the first years after independence, the Government chose not to rely on financial benefits for social assistance, but offered non-cash benefits to households, often in an ad hoc manner. After the conflicts of 2006-07, the approach to social protection changed as the National Recovery Strategy concentrated efforts in five areas: transitional shelter and housing; social protection; security and stability; local socio-economic development; and confidence-building/reconciliation activities. As a consequence, the mentioned set of social provisions was created to lower

---

[35] *Sucos* are the smallest administrative units in the State, comparable to a hamlet or small village.

tensions and to promote social peace. The social protection package launched in 2008 included SAII, veteran benefits and the Bolsa da Mãe programmes. The rapid increase in beneficiaries and coverage led to large increases in social expenditures, from $109 million in 2008 to $160 million in 2012.

Overcoming constraints: For a country with such limited infrastructure, the rapid increase in pension coverage is an impressive feat. Currently, SAII covers almost 87,000 older persons, a number that corresponds to 103 per cent of the population above the age of 60 in Timor-Leste. However, coverage of persons with disabilities remains a challenge. It is estimated that there are about 40,000 persons living with physical or mental disabilities in the country and that SAII reaches only 7,313 of them – about 18.2 per cent of the target population.

As mentioned earlier, the lack of financial infrastructure in the districts and the difficulties in accessing isolated communities result in payments being made only twice per year. A solution for this is being developed in two manners: the first is to progressively require the use of bank accounts to receive benefits (current limitations are due to fragile banking infrastructure in the districts), and the second is to use mobile units for payments. The mobile payment system – currently running on a pilot basis – is designed for beneficiaries with mobility problems or who are sick.

Other issues arise from problems with documents and the identification of beneficiaries. Many Timor-Leste citizens do not have identity documents. Among those who do, the most common identity document is the electoral card. This creates three challenges. The first challenge is to identify those who do not have any documents. Many do not have documents either because they have never had them or because they were lost during displacement due to conflicts. The *Suco* chiefs often intervene in these cases to attest an applicant's identity. The second issue is that the electoral card is easily falsified, leading to cases of fraud, which can partly explain the coverage of older persons being above 100 per cent. Lastly, the lack of documentation extends to death certificates, which are often not issued. Thus, payments could still be made to family members of beneficiaries whose deaths are not reported.

Improving coverage among people with disabilities goes beyond the improvement of identifying and registering beneficiaries. Families are often ashamed of having a member with a disability, and thus hide them from outsiders, including social workers and survey collectors. For coverage among this group to increase, people with disabilities need to be perceived as individuals with the same rights and needs as everyone else. In this sense, the Government is investing in raising awareness and social inclusion of persons with disabilities.

Additionally, despite the high coverage of older people, the value of the benefit paid has not been adjusted since 2010. Inflation during this period has reduced the purchasing power of the transfer and has likely reduced the impact of the Programme. Indexation mechanisms could be adopted to help guarantee that the pension remains at an adequate level to support older persons and people with disabilities in their subsistence.

4. What is the main impact on people's lives?

Outcomes: The old-age pension achieved universal coverage early on and continues to maintain high coverage rates. There are few studies on the effective impacts of the pension. However, a 2011 simulation estimated that SAII reduced national poverty from 54 to 49 per cent and poverty among older persons from 55.1 to 37.6 per cent.[36] For persons with disabilities, reduction in the poverty headcount was 17.5 percentage points, from 63.3 to 45.8 per cent.

---

[36] At the international poverty line of $1.25 per capita per day.

Impact on people's lives: Although older persons over 60 years of age represent only 6 per cent of the population, almost one in three households have an older person in residence. Information on the use of SAII benefits shows that recipients spend most of the transfer (88.4 per cent of the benefit value) on food items, followed by frequent expenditures on education (28.1 per cent of recipients), showing that inter-generational transfers are common. Other uses of the benefit include health care (13.4 per cent) and purchase of livestock or other assets (6.4 per cent). The use of the benefits shows that older persons contribute to overall household economies and invest a significant share of their resources into improving household earning capacity.

Figure 26: SAII budget evolution in Timor-Leste, 2008-15

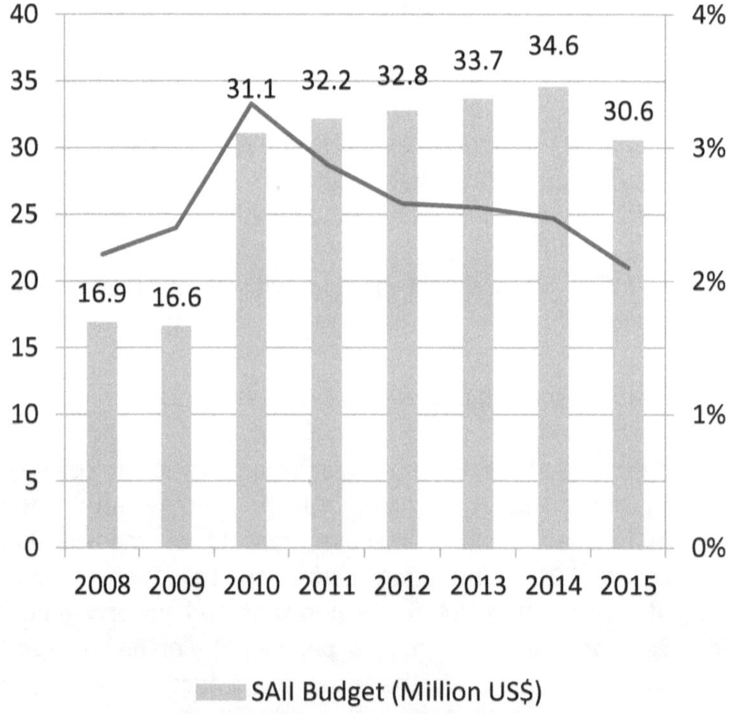

SAII Budget (Million US$)

Source: Ministry of Social Solidarity, Directorate for Social Security; World Bank Database.

Sustainability of the system: The cost of SAII has varied from $30 to $35 million in the last few years, just above 2 per cent of non-oil GDP. This will most likely change in the future since life expectancy is increasing rapidly in Timor-Leste, rising from 60.2 years in 2001 to 68.2 in 2014. Thus, more beneficiaries will receive the transfers and for longer periods of time. However, the creation of a non-cumulative contributory old-age pension scheme will result in broader coverage than the Transitory Social Security Scheme, which will reduce the number people depending on SAII. Nonetheless, dependency ratios of older persons will continue to be low for many decades to come since the Timorese birth rate remains one of the highest in the world.

5. What's next?

Plenty of challenges remain to improve the reach and effectiveness of SAII. In order to learn more about its impact, an evaluation study is being developed. This will bring to light the true impact of SAII and ways in which its operations and benefits can be improved. Parallel to this, efforts to improve the registration and payment systems, and to raise awareness among the Timorese people to increase coverage of the disability pension, are at the top of the MSS' agenda.

These improvements will, unquestionably, help the SAII to overcome some of its limitations; however, it is important to highlight the achievements the SAII has had so far. Even in places with little to no infrastructure, it is possible to reach most of the eligible people. Moreover, the Timorese experience shows that universal social protection programmes are affordable and can have significant impacts on the lives of the beneficiaries and their families.

6. References

Dale, P.; Lepuschuetz, L.; Umapathi, N. 2014. "Peace, prosperity and safety nets in Timor-Leste: Competing priorities or complementary investments?" in Asia & the Pacific Policy Studies, Vol. 1, No. 2, pp. 287-296.

Democratic Republic of Timor-Leste. 2002. Constitution of the Democratic Republic of Timor-Leste (Dili).

—. 2002. National Development Plan (Dili).

—. 2008. Decreto-Lei N.º 19/2008 de 19 de Junho - Subsidio de Apoio a idosos e Inválidos (Dili).

—. 2010. Diploma Ministerial Conjunto/MSS/MF/2010 de 25 de agosto - Aumenta o montante do Subsídio de Apoio a Idosos e Inválidos (Dili).

—. 2011. Timor-Leste Strategic Development Plan 2011-2030 (Dili).

—. 2012. 10 anos depois: O Contributo dos Programas Sociais na Construção de um Estado Social em Timor-Leste (Dili).

ILO. 2014. Pensions and other social protection benefits for older persons: Insights from the ILO World Social Protection Report 2014/15, Social Protection for All Policy Brief No. 3/2014 (Geneva).

Kent, L.; Wallis, J. 2014. Timor-Leste's Veterans' Pension Scheme: Who are the Beneficiaries and Who is Missing Out?

Umapathi, N.; Dale, P.; Lepuschuetz, L. 2013. Timor-Leste-Social assistance public expenditure and program performance report (No. 73484) (Washington, DC, The World Bank).

World Bank. 2014. Creation of a reformed pension system for civil servants in Timor-Leste (Washington, DC).

16

Trinidad and Tobago: Universal pension[37]

Trinidad and Tobago is ranked highly in terms of human development, which is evident from its ranking at number 64 in the Human Development Index. While the country has performed creditably in the last decade, there was a decline in 2015 and future economic performance is being challenged. GDP growth and revenue mainly come from the energy sector (oil and gas) and related companies; therefore, the country is not immune to the challenges posed to oil-based economies.

The latest official poverty rate according to the 2005 Survey of Living Conditions was 16.7 per cent, with 1.2 per cent of the population identified as extremely poor (indigent) and another 9 per cent vulnerable to poverty (Kairi Consultants Ltd., 2007). While the 2014 Survey of Living Conditions will disclose precise up-to-date poverty figures, preliminary findings have already pointed to an increase in the poverty rate. There is no official poverty line in Trinidad and Tobago. The 2011 Census indicated that the country had an ageing population. A total of 58 per cent of older persons fell within the 60-69 age group and the age group of 80 years and over was also growing. The data further revealed the feminization of ageing.

---

[37] This chapter was authored by Vijay Gangapersad of the Ministry of Social Development and Family Services in Trinidad and Tobago and Ariel Pino of the ILO and reviewed by Isabel Ortiz of the ILO. It was first published in September 2016.

Table 7: Population of Trinidad and Tobago (in thousands)

	2010	2015	2020
Total	1,328	1,360	1,378
60-64	55	65	75
65-69	42	49	58
70+	68	79	94
Total 60+	165	193	227
60+ / Total	12.4%	14.2%	16.5%

Source: United Nations, Department of Economic and Social Affairs, Population Division, 2015.

In Trinidad and Tobago, the Government plays a major role in the social protection landscape. The Government provides a very comprehensive suite of services for older persons aimed at managing the various risks associated with this cohort. Poor health, a major risk associated with older persons, is adequately addressed by the Ministry of Health (MoH).

1. Main lessons learned

At least in principle, the combination of the National Insurance Board (NIB) pension and the Senior Citizens' Pension (SCP) is considered to be universal. Everyone aged 65 and older is entitled to a benefit. Even if someone does not contribute sufficiently to qualify under the contributory scheme, the individual can rely on a SCP from age 65, provided compliance with some residency criteria.

Old-age pensions follow a rights-based approach and are included in national acts. Universal free health access and a wide range of services are available to old-age persons. Trinidad and Tobago provides benefits and services that fulfil the social protection floor for old-age persons, which requires:
- access to a nationally defined set of goods and services, including essential health care; and
- basic income security, at least at a nationally defined minimum level, for older persons.

2. What does the system look like?

The social protection system in Trinidad and Tobago has undergone significant modifications in the number and scope of services offered to older persons. Today, however, the system operates in very much the same way as it did in earlier years, consisting of contributory and non-contributory schemes, including universal health access through public health facilities. The social insurance and social assistance programmes continue to provide income security for older persons in Trinidad and Tobago. The National Insurance Board (NIB) administers the social insurance scheme and the Social Welfare Division (SWD) of the Ministry of Social Development and Family Services (MSDFS) manages the social assistance programmes. There is also a wide range of services provided to old-age persons.

Universal access to free health care at health clinics and hospitals, as well as the provision of selected drugs at no cost, are guaranteed under the Chronic Disease Assistance Programme (CDAP). The CDAP is managed by the Ministry of Health and provides citizens with free prescription drugs and other pharmaceutical items to combat a number of diseases, including diabetes, cardiac diseases, arthritis, glaucoma, mental depression, high blood pressure, benign prostatic hyperplasia, hypercholesterolemia, Parkinson's disease and thyroid diseases. When prescription medication is not available at the public health dispensary, dispensary services are available under the Ministry of Social Development and Family Services. Accessibility and coverage are not issues associated with the health-care system since the public offerings are usually complemented by subsidized services from the private sector when necessary.

Loneliness, one of the major risks facing older persons, is managed through the Senior Centres Programme, which was designed to bring older persons together so that they expand their social capital. The programme, which targets older persons who are in good health and physically active, is designed to provide the necessary physical, social and mental stimulation, as well as support mechanisms, to enable older persons to optimize their later years. Centres are administered by non-governmental organizations (NGOs) and/or community-based organizations (CBOs), with financial support from the Government. Elderly and Differently Abled Mobile (ELDAMO) provides free transportation to older persons to go about their daily routine. Free transportation on the public service transport system (bus rides, ferry to Tobago and trips on water taxis during non-peak hours) is also available to all older persons in Trinidad and Tobago.

Homelessness is another risk associated with growing old. The Homes for Older Persons Act provides oversight of Residential Homes for older persons as well as the regulation and monitoring of all facilities for older persons in Trinidad and Tobago. Housing opportunities are also available under the State, such as the Pensioners Quarters, as part of the support for older persons. Other subsidized housing programmes are also available to older persons.

The Geriatric Adolescent Partnership Programme and the Retirees Adolescent Partnership Programme bridge the generation gap and allow older persons to interact with younger persons and provide mutual support to each other. Older persons also benefit from a number of public programmes and aid, such as free transportation and caregiving services (means-tested services provided through the Geriatric Adolescent Partnership Programme). Several other means-tested programmes are available to older persons, such as: subsidies on annual water and electricity rates; public education; a home improvement grant programme (aid for needy citizens whose houses were substandard, dilapidated or in need of repair); house rental grants; household furniture and appliances; and home care and assistive devices.

The Older Persons Information Center (OPIC) was established by the Ministry of Social Development and Family Services to serve as a referral facility for information on resources, services and products for older persons. Social programmes for older persons that treat poor health, homelessness and loneliness continue to have relevance in Trinidad and Tobago. These are some of the social situations confronting older persons which the Government seeks to address through various initiatives.

Table 8: Pension system in Trinidad and Tobago

	Social pension	Contributory pension	Health coverage
Institutions	MSDFS	NIB, Ministry of Finance (supervision)	MoH, CEDAP
Benefits	SCP Social services	Old-age pension, old-age grant, survivorship, invalidity	Health care, drugs
Beneficiaries	Aged 60 or more, means-tested	Employed persons, domestic workers	Universal

Benefit packages: The NIB retirement pension is paid at age 60 to anyone who has been insured with a minimum of 750 weeks of contributions. A retirement grant in the form of a one-time lump-sum payment is paid to those insured persons who have made less than 750 weekly contributions. The overall contribution rate is 13.2 per cent (4.4 per cent employees and 8.8 per cent employers) and the maximum insurable earnings is 13,600 Trinidadian dollars (TTD) per month. Contributions are paid according to 16 wage classes. The self-employed are not covered under the NIB.

The NIB pension is calculated based on the categories in which contributions have been paid. An average rate of contribution is calculated by considering all the contributions paid. The earnings class to which this average rate corresponds is the class in which the benefit will be paid. The minimum monthly pension is TTD3,000 (approximately US$445), which represents 115 per cent of the minimum wage established at TTD2,600 (approximately $388) per month. Current pensioners receiving the minimum pension represent 97 per cent of the total beneficiaries.

Table 9: NIB beneficiaries and expenditure in Trinidad and Tobago

Beneficiaries	2013	2014	2015
Long-term	132,253	137,481	144,804
Short-term	32,207	30,805	32,804
Total	164,660	168,286	177,608
Benefit expenditures (billions of TTD)	3.56	3.92	4.22

Source: National Insurance Board, 2016.

Table 10: Long-term benefits and expenditure in Trinidad and Tobago, 2015

	Beneficiaries	% of total long-term benefits	Expenditure (million TTD)	(% of total)
Retirement pension	96,395	66.57	3,362.09	86.10
Retirement grant	4,568	3.15	139.15	3.56
*Survivor benefit	39,644	27.38	329.01	8.43
Invalidity pension	4,197	2.90	74.62	1.91
Total	144,804	100.00	3,904.87	100.00
% of total beneficiaries	81.53			

* Survivor benefit and grant. Source: National Insurance Board, 2016.

The SWD administers the Senior Citizens' Pension (SCP) (formerly Old Age Pension), in accordance with the Senior Citizens' Pension Act Chapter 32:02. The SCP is a monthly grant paid to persons aged 65 or more based on their income and residential status. SCP recipients must be resident in Trinidad and Tobago for 20 years preceding the date of application. Any periods of absence must not exceed five years in the aggregate during the 20 years preceding the application. SCP recipients must also have spent a period of at least fifty (50) years total in the country to be eligible for the benefit.

Table 11: Senior Citizen's Pension in Trinidad and Tobago and beneficiaries, 2016

	Senior Income		Senior Citizens' Pension		Beneficiaries in August 2016
TTD	TTD	US$	TTD	US$	
0-1,500.00	0 - 224		3,500	522	66,021
1,500.01 -2000	225 – 299		3,000	448	1,407
2,000.01 -2,500	300 – 373		2,500	373	417
2500.01- 3,000	374 – 448		2,000	299	19,342
3,000.01 - 3,500	449 – 522		1,500	224	1339
3,500.01 -4,000	523 – 597		1,000	149	1129
4000.01 - 4,500	598 - 672		500	75	303

Source: Social Welfare Division, 2016.

Figure 27: Recipients of Trinidad and Tobago's Senior Citizen's Pension, 2001-16

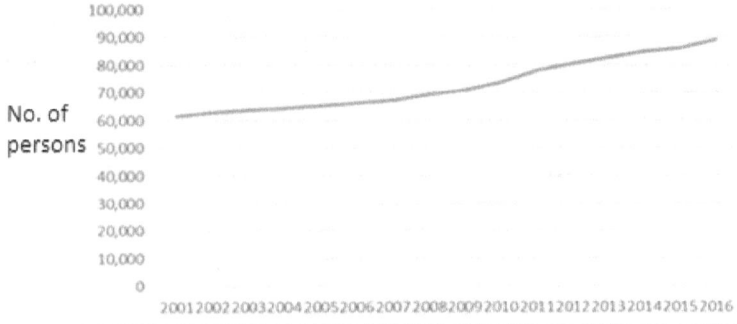

Source: Department of Social Welfare, 2016.

Coverage has expanded significantly over the years. In 2001, just over 61,000 persons received the Senior Citizens' Pension. In 2015, 6,694 new beneficiaries were added to the system. As of

September 2016, a total of 90,800 senior citizens were in receipt of the SCP.

In 2000, the SCP benefit amount was between TTD620 and TTD720 per month. This has risen steadily over the years with the maximum SCP now TTD3,500 per month with 74.21 per cent of the recipients receiving this amount. The amount being paid is greater than the established poverty line and significantly above the indigence line. The sum when calculated also exceeds the established minimum wage for the country. Where there are two persons living in the same household (husband and wife) who qualify for the SCP, they are guaranteed to have a minimum guaranteed household income of TTD7,000 per month. If they have other private income, they are likely to have an income of TTD10,000.

This steady increase in the amount of persons receiving the pension is the result of successive administrations implementing responsive policy changes for this target group. Existing since 1939, the Government has continuously enhanced the benefit levels and other criteria associated with this grant so as to make it more responsive to the needs of older persons. One of the major changes responsible for the increased coverage is the statutory income limit to qualify for a pension. Today, a person can have personal income of up to TTD4,500 and still qualify for a sum under the non-contributory SCP. Some of the changes made over the years are listed in Table 12.

Table 12: Evolution of the SCP in Trinidad and Tobago in recent years

Previous Provisions	Changes	Remarks
Senior Citizens' Pension(Legislation)		
Senior Citizens' Grant	Senior Citizens' Pension	Allowed pensioners psychological comfort and peace of mind

TTD720 maximum payable benefit (Year 2000)	TTD3,500 maximum payable benefit	Allowed greater purchasing power thereby improving the quality of life
Interest from savings account was used as income, thereby denying persons who had savings	Interest from savings accounts is no longer used in the calculation of income.	This new measure created an incentive for older persons to save.
Income calculated on an annual basis. This measure resulted in persons being denied pension when they received one-off payments that was in excess of a fixed amount even if they had no income.	Income calculated on a monthly basis	This measure allowed the pension to be determined based on real monthly income.
Statutory limit from as low as TTD5,000 annually to TTD33,600 annually. In the past assets were also used.	New statutory limit of TTD4,500 per month.	Only real monthly income is used in the calculation of the Senior Citizens' Pension. More people can now qualify for the SCP.
One-off lump-sum payments used in the calculation of income. This	In the calculation of the Senior Citizens' Pension, lump-sum payments shall not be	This measure allowed people to save rather than spend their

prevented people from qualifying for pensions in the year payments were received.	taken into account.	money to be able to qualify for SCP
Persons must have resided in Trinidad and Tobago for 60 years in total in order to qualify for the Senior Citizens' Pension	Persons who reside in Trinidad and Tobago at least 50 years can receive the pension.	This change benefitted citizens who were born in the country.
All periods spent out of the country used in the calculation of period abroad.	In the calculation of ordinary residence in Trinidad, the following have been exempted: • Where the person was abroad for the purpose of employment for a firm registered in Trinidad and Tobago or a company incorporated in Trinidad and Tobago • Where the person was abroad in the service of the Government of Trinidad and Tobago It is to be noted that this also applies to the dependants of such a person.	Person who spent time abroad in the development of the country was penalized for being out of the country. This includes a number of persons who had to serve at missions or represent the country in sports or otherwise.

Financing: The SCP programme is national in nature and is financed directly from the National Budget. The many changes made to the policy over the years have resulted in a significant increase in the expenditures associated with the SCP. While in 2001 the expenditures were TTD548,368,305, in 2015 the expenditures increased to TTD2,647,056,180 (1.6 per cent of GDP). For fiscal year 2016/17, the sum allocated for this programme is TTD3,319,554,016. Already, it appears as though additional funds will be required. The evolution of programme expenditures is described in Table 13.

Table 13: Expenditure for select social assistance programmes in Trinidad and Tobago (TTD and % of GDP)

	Estimated for 2015	
	In TTD	% of GDP
Community-based Environment Protection & Enhancement Programme (CEPEP)	606,200,000	0.37
Disability Assistance Grant(DAG)	379,506,550	0.23
Government Assistance for Tertiary Expenses (GATE)	712,000,000	0.43
National Schools Dietary Services Limited	250,000,000	0.15
On the Job Training (OJT) Programme	308,000,000	0.19
Public Assistance Grant (PAG)	409,500,000	0.25
Senior Citizens' Pension (SCP)	**2,861,470,500**	**1.73**
Target Conditional Cash Transfer Programme (Food Support Programme)	294,000,000	0.18
Unemployment Relief Programme (URP)	717,500,000	0.43
TOTAL	**6,538,177,050**	**3.96**

Source: Social Sector Investment Programme 2016 – Central Bank.

Figure 28: Expenditure under the SCP programme in Trinidad and Tobago, TTD

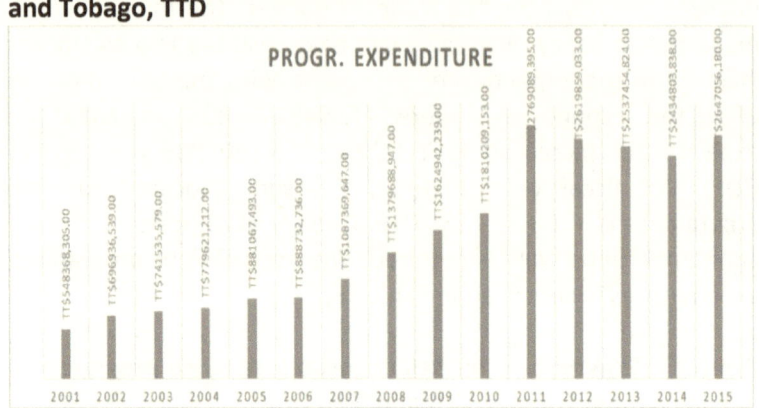

Source: Social Welfare Department, 2016.

Legal aspects: NIB benefits are regulated by the National Insurance Act, updated 31 December 2014. The SCP is regulated by the Senior Citizens' Pension Act, updated 31 December 2014.

Two pieces of legislation continue to guide the operations of the Social Welfare Division and the administration of the Public Assistance Grant and the Senior Citizens' Pension.

1. The Public Assistance Act, Chapter 32:03, provides for the establishment of the Central and Local Public Assistance Boards to administer the Old Age Pension, Public Assistance, Disability Assistance and Urgent Temporary Assistance, as well as for the maintenance of the various registers and accounting records in their districts.

2. The Central Public Assistance Board has the responsibility for general policy guidance and considers appeals made in connection with any decisions made by the Local Public Assistance Boards. The Local Boards enquire generally into the conditions of the poor and consider applications for the Senior Citizens' Pension (Formerly Old Age Pension), Public Assistance and Disability Assistance Grants. The Central Board is comprised of eight members, while the Local Public

Assistance Boards have five members each. Members are appointed by the Cabinet following nominations made by the Minister in accordance with Sections 4 and 8 of the Act.

Institutional arrangements for delivery: To receive the SCP, an application form must be submitted to the Local Board Office of the respective district. Applicants may be required to attend an assessment meeting with the Local Public Assistance Board, which decides on all applications. Persons whose applications have been rejected have the right to appeal. There are 11 Local Public Assistance Boards covering the country. As of September 2016, 90,800 senior citizens were in receipt of the SCP. Of this total, 9,058 were new beneficiaries.

The SCP is paid via direct deposit into the recipient's personal bank account or by cheques mailed directly to the recipient's address. The Ministry launched a biometric card system in 2015 and this is expected to be the platform for the Central Beneficiary Registry. This system allows for enhanced identity verification and identity fraud reduction. Enrolment of persons commenced in July 2014.

3. How was this major breakthrough achieved?

The provision of welfare services dates back to the colonial era and was largely an effort of civil society organizations. The labour disturbances in the late-1930s led to the first official form of social assistance, emanating from recommendations from the Moyne West India Commission. The Commission drew attention to the fact that it was essential to have a well-defined programme of social welfare and that the programme should be part of overall government policy. It was not until 1938 that the existing services were grouped together for more effective impact and control, and in July 1939 the Department of Social Welfare was inaugurated to administer Social Assistance and the Old Age Pension.

A report by the Pan American Health Organization (PAHO) (1989) notes that in Trinidad and Tobago the most important issues that confront older persons aged 60 years and over in their daily lives pertained to economic and health matters. The study also found that older persons' basic needs were not being adequately met by their financial situation (PAHO, 1989). A survey by Camejo (1999) also found that older persons had concerns about their declining health and their ability to go on performing activities related to daily living. The report contends that poverty has a relevant age dimension where both needs and income potentially change over the life cycle.

Upon retirement, older persons are now required to live on fixed incomes that are constituted from pensions and assets accumulated over their lifetimes. In many instances, older persons continue to function as the heads of households and their incomes represent the only steady flow of resources for the support of large and extended families. The fact that the working age population of 16-45 year olds is shrinking suggests that older persons will be left to fend for themselves. In a study carried out by Rawlins et al. (2008), 33 per cent of surveyed older persons felt lonely despite only 16 per cent living alone.

4. What are the main impacts on people's lives?

Many of the challenges faced by older persons are related to their stage of development and are irreversible. As such, necessary support systems are required so that older persons can cope with the many risks associated with growing old. Major risks associated with growing old include retirement, unemployment and employability. A well-defined and functioning pension system is available to manage the impacts of such risks. The pension system in Trinidad and Tobago is categorized in three layers with the first layer being the non-contributory Senior Citizens Pension for persons 65 years of age or older and whose income is below a certain threshold. The second and third layers are risk mitigating strategies in the form of government mandates for social insurance and occupational pensions. Occupational pension plans are also offered by some employers in the private sector, and public sector pensions are provided to all employees paid monthly. A wide range of services provides support to old-age persons.

Impacts on people's lives: Pensions in Trinidad and Tobago have extensive coverage. The World Bank cited that Trinidad and Tobago had almost reached universal pension coverage. Their report cited that over 80 per cent of persons 65 years and older are receiving the non-contributory pension, while in the social insurance scheme administered by the National Insurance Board, 73 per cent of persons 60 years or older are covered and receiving long-term benefits.

In terms of adequacy, benefit levels of the various grants far exceed the poverty threshold. Additionally, the system adopts a concept similar to that of the social protection floor: a guaranteed base (TTD3,000 per month) complemented by benefits from other systems, where older persons can invest and extend the scope, level and quality of benefits provided beyond this base.

5. What's next?

Trinidad and Tobago is under fiscal pressure because of the economic slowdown generated by the adverse international context and low oil and gas prices. Fiscal consolidation has started and public institutions are operating under reduced budgets (i.e. 7 per cent reduction in 2015). This situation is likely to continue in light of the expected negative 2 per cent GDP growth for 2016. Diversification of the economy is high on the political agenda to ensure long-term economic growth and sustainability. Despite this adverse context, the Government is expected to increase budget allocations towards social infrastructure and programming by 1.2 per cent in 2016 compared to 2015.

Other challenges are related to the efficiency and effectiveness of existing programmes, as well as to the right incentives that social programmes should provide. The Ministry of Social Development and Family Services (MSDFS) is fully implementing the Biometric Card System and establishing an integrated information technology (IT) system. The objective of the system is to facilitate the modernization and effective delivery of social services. The system would automate and re-engineer the MSDFS's core business processes, operational activities, business and programme performance, thereby providing an integrated approach to case management. It is expected that there would be a seamless administration of social services together with data and information collaboration among Government ministries and agencies. Other developments proposed by the MSDFS are:

- develop the National Plan of Action on Ageing for Trinidad and Tobago;
- develop Residential Long-Term Care Facilities in collaboration with Ministry of Health;
- revamp the Senior Citizens Bureau (i.e., Skills Bank and Placement Agency);
- develop Omnibus Legislation to allow for entry and investigations into the living conditions of the elderly in their private domiciles;
- review the National Policy on Ageing;
- assist in the formulation of the National Policy on the Family to address the elderly within the context of the family;
- establish age-friendly health-care facilities;
- establish standards for universal accessibility to public buildings for the elderly and persons with disabilities;
- launch a public education campaign on ageing to include inter-generational initiatives; and
- conduct public awareness campaigns to promote the Chronic Disease Assistance Programme (CDAP), free bus, water taxi and ferry rides and free cataract surgery.

The linkages between contributory and non-contributory schemes in the areas of benefit design, administration, financing, delivery of services and administrative tools have to be reinforced. The NIB has to consider the implementation of social protection mechanisms for the self-employed and the unemployed. Such protection schemes will have considerable impacts in the long run by reducing the number of social assistance benefits that would have to be paid in the future.

The forthcoming results of the 2014 Survey of Living Conditions will provide invaluable information about poverty levels in Trinidad and Tobago, particularly in comparison to poverty levels previously registered in 2005. It will also allow for further analysis of the adequacy and coverage of old-age benefits.

6. References

Camejo, A. 1999. *The elderly in Trinidad and Tobago* (Port of Spain, Ministry of Social Development).

Kairi Consultants Ltd. 2007. *Analysis of the 2005 Survey of Living Conditions for Trinidad and Tobago* (Tunapuna).

The Government of the Republic of Trinidad and Tobago. 2014a. National Insurance Act, updated 31 December 2014. Available at:
http://rgd.legalaffairs.gov.tt/laws2/alphabetical_list/lawspdfs/3 2.01.pdf.

—. 2014b. Senior Citizens' Pension Act, updated 31 December 2014.
Available at:
http://rgd.legalaffairs.gov.tt/laws2/alphabetical_list/lawspdfs/3 2.02.pdf.

Ministry of Finance. 2014. *Social Sector Investment Programme 2015* (Port of Spain). Available at:

http://www.finance.gov.tt/social-sector-investment-programme-2015/.

Ministry of Social Development and Family Services, Social Welfare Division. 2016. www.mpsd.gov.tt.

National Insurance Board. 2016. www.nibtt.net.

Pan American Health Organization (PAHO). 1989. *A profile of the elderly in Trinidad and Tobago*, PAHO Technical Paper No. 22 1989 (Washington, DC, PAHO).
Rawlins, J.M.; Simeon, D.T.; Ramdath, D.D., Chadee, D.D. 2008. "The elderly in Trinidad: Health, social and economic status and issues of loneliness", in *West Indian Medical Journal*, Vol. 57, No. 6, pp. 589-95.

Rofman, R.; Apella, I.; Vezza, E. 2015. *Beyond contributory pensions: Fourteen experiences with coverage expansion in Latin America. Directions in Development--Human Development* (Washington, DC, World Bank).

United Nations Department of Economic and Social Affairs, Population Division. 2015. *World Population Prospects: The 2015 Revision* (New York).

United National Development Programme. *Human Development Report 2015* (New York).

Annex 1: Social Protection Floors Recommendation, 2012 (No. 202)

PREAMBLE

The General Conference of the International Labour Organization,

Having been convened at Geneva by the Governing Body of the International Labour Office, and having met in its 101st Session on 30 May 2012, and

Reaffirming that the right to social security is a human right, and

Acknowledging that the right to social security is, along with promoting employment, an economic and social necessity for development and progress, and

Recognizing that social security is an important tool to prevent and reduce poverty, inequality, social exclusion and social insecurity, to promote equal opportunity and gender and racial equality, and to support the transition from informal to formal employment, and

Considering that social security is an investment in people that empowers them to adjust to changes in the economy and in the labour market, and that social security systems act as automatic social and economic stabilizers, help stimulate aggregate demand in times of crisis and beyond, and help support a transition to a more sustainable economy, and

Considering that the prioritization of policies aimed at sustainable long-term growth associated with social inclusion helps overcome extreme poverty and reduces social inequalities and differences within and among regions, and

Recognizing that the transition to formal employment and the establishment of sustainable social security systems are mutually supportive, and

Recalling that the Declaration of Philadelphia recognizes the solemn obligation of the International Labour Organization to contribute to "achiev[ing] ... the extension of social security measures to provide a basic income to all in need of such protection and comprehensive medical care", and

Considering the Universal Declaration of Human Rights, in particular Articles 22 and 25, and the International Covenant on Economic, Social and Cultural Rights, in particular Articles 9, 11 and 12, and

Considering also ILO social security standards, in particular the Social Security (Minimum Standards) Convention, 1952 (No. 102), the Income Security Recommendation, 1944 (No. 67), and the Medical Care Recommendation, 1944 (No. 69), and noting that these standards are of continuing relevance and continue to be important references for social security systems, and

Recalling that the ILO Declaration on Social Justice for a Fair Globalization recognizes that "the commitments and efforts of Members and the Organization to implement the ILO's constitutional mandate, including through international labour standards, and to place full and productive employment and decent work at the centre of economic and social policies, should be based on ... (ii) developing and enhancing measures of social protection ... which are sustainable and adapted to national circumstances, including ... the extension of social security to all", and

Considering the resolution and Conclusions concerning the recurrent discussion on social protection (social security) adopted by the International Labour Conference at its 100th Session (2011), which recognize the need for a Recommendation complementing existing ILO social security standards and providing guidance to Members in building social protection floors tailored to national circumstances and levels of development, as part of comprehensive social security systems, and

Having decided upon the adoption of certain proposals with regard to social protection floors, which are the subject of the fourth item on the agenda of the session, and

Having determined that these proposals shall take the form of a Recommendation; adopts this fourteenth day of June of the year two thousand and twelve the following Recommendation, which may be cited as the Social Protection Floors Recommendation, 2012.

I. OBJECTIVES, SCOPE AND PRINCIPLES

1. This Recommendation provides guidance to Members to:
    a. establish and maintain, as applicable, social protection floors as a fundamental element of their national social security systems; and
    b. implement social protection floors within strategies for the extension of social security that progressively ensure higher levels of social security to as many people as possible, guided by ILO social security standards.
2. For the purpose of this Recommendation, social protection floors are nationally defined sets of basic social security guarantees which secure protection aimed at preventing or alleviating poverty, vulnerability and social exclusion.
3. Recognizing the overall and primary responsibility of the State in giving effect to this Recommendation, Members should apply the following principles:
    a. universality of protection, based on social solidarity;
    b. entitlement to benefits prescribed by national law;
    c. adequacy and predictability of benefits;
    d. non-discrimination, gender equality and responsiveness to special needs;
    e. social inclusion, including of persons in the informal economy;
    f. respect for the rights and dignity of people covered by the social security guarantees;
    g. progressive realization, including by setting targets and time frames;
    h. solidarity in financing while seeking to achieve an optimal balance between the responsibilities and interests among those who finance and benefit from social security schemes;
    i. consideration of diversity of methods and approaches, including of financing mechanisms and delivery systems;

    j. transparent, accountable and sound financial management and administration;

    k. financial, fiscal and economic sustainability with due regard to social justice and equity;

    l. coherence with social, economic and employment policies;

    m. coherence across institutions responsible for delivery of social protection;

    n. high-quality public services that enhance the delivery of social security systems;

    o. efficiency and accessibility of complaint and appeal procedures;

    p. regular monitoring of implementation, and periodic evaluation;

    q. full respect for collective bargaining and freedom of association for all workers; and

    r. tripartite participation with representative organizations of employers and workers, as well as consultation with other relevant and representative organizations of persons concerned.

II. NATIONAL SOCIAL PROTECTION FLOORS

4. Members should, in accordance with national circumstances, establish as quickly as possible and maintain their social protection floors comprising basic social security guarantees. The guarantees should ensure at a minimum that, over the life cycle, all in need have access to essential health care and to basic income security which together secure effective access to goods and services defined as necessary at the national level.

5. The social protection floors referred to in Paragraph 4 should comprise at least the following basic social security guarantees:

    a. access to a nationally defined set of goods and services, constituting essential health care, including maternity care, that meets the criteria of availability, accessibility, acceptability and quality;

    b.   basic income security for children, at least at a nationally defined minimum level, providing access to nutrition, education, care and any other necessary goods and services;

    c.   basic income security, at least at a nationally defined minimum level, for persons in active age who are unable to earn sufficient income, in particular in cases of sickness, unemployment, maternity and disability; and

    d.   basic income security, at least at a nationally defined minimum level, for older persons.

6.   Subject to their existing international obligations, Members should provide the basic social security guarantees referred to in this Recommendation to at least all residents and children, as defined in national laws and regulations.

7.   Basic social security guarantees should be established by law. National laws and regulations should specify the range, qualifying conditions and levels of the benefits giving effect to these guarantees. Impartial, transparent, effective, simple, rapid, accessible and inexpensive complaint and appeal procedures should also be specified. Access to complaint and appeal procedures should be free of charge to the applicant. Systems should be in place that enhance compliance with national legal frameworks.

8.   When defining the basic social security guarantees, Members should give due consideration to the following:

    a.   persons in need of health care should not face hardship and an increased risk of poverty due to the financial consequences of accessing essential health care. Free prenatal and postnatal medical care for the most vulnerable should also be considered;

    b.   basic income security should allow life in dignity. Nationally defined minimum levels of income may correspond to the monetary value of a set of necessary goods and services, national poverty lines, income thresholds for social assistance or other comparable thresholds established by national law or practice, and may take into account regional differences;

    c. the levels of basic social security guarantees should be regularly reviewed through a transparent procedure that is established by national laws, regulations or practice, as appropriate; and

    d. in regard to the establishment and review of the levels of these guarantees, tripartite participation with representative organizations of employers and workers, as well as consultation with other relevant and representative organizations of persons concerned, should be ensured.

9.

    1. In providing the basic social security guarantees, Members should consider different approaches with a view to implementing the most effective and efficient combination of benefits and schemes in the national context.

    2. Benefits may include child and family benefits, sickness and health-care benefits, maternity benefits, disability benefits, old-age benefits, survivors' benefits, unemployment benefits and employment guarantees, and employment injury benefits as well as any other social benefits in cash or in kind.

    3. Schemes providing such benefits may include universal benefit schemes, social insurance schemes, social assistance schemes, negative income tax schemes, public employment schemes and employment support schemes.

10. In designing and implementing national social protection floors, Members should:

    a. combine preventive, promotional and active measures, benefits and social services;

    b. promote productive economic activity and formal employment through considering policies that include public procurement, government credit provisions, labour inspection, labour market policies and tax incentives, and that promote education, vocational training, productive skills and employability; and

    c. ensure coordination with other policies that enhance formal employment, income generation, education, literacy, vocational training, skills and employability, that reduce precariousness, and that promote secure work, entrepreneurship and sustainable enterprises within a decent work framework.

11.

    1. Members should consider using a variety of different methods to mobilize the necessary resources to ensure financial, fiscal and economic sustainability of national social protection floors, taking into account the contributory capacities of different population groups. Such methods may include, individually or in combination, effective enforcement of tax and contribution obligations, reprioritizing expenditure, or a broader and sufficiently progressive revenue base.

    2. In applying such methods, Members should consider the need to implement measures to prevent fraud, tax evasion and non-payment of contributions.

12. National social protection floors should be financed by national resources. Members whose economic and fiscal capacities are insufficient to implement the guarantees may seek international cooperation and support that complement their own efforts.

III. NATIONAL STRATEGIES FOR THE EXTENSION OF SOCIAL SECURITY

13.

    1. Members should formulate and implement national social security extension strategies, based on national consultations through effective social dialogue and social participation. National strategies should:

        a. prioritize the implementation of social protection floors as a starting point for countries that do not have a minimum level of social security guarantees, and as a fundamental element of their national social security systems; and

      b. seek to provide higher levels of protection to as many people as possible, reflecting economic and fiscal capacities of Members, and as soon as possible.

  2. For this purpose, Members should progressively build and maintain comprehensive and adequate social security systems coherent with national policy objectives and seek to coordinate social security policies with other public policies.

14. When formulating and implementing national social security extension strategies, Members should:

    a. set objectives reflecting national priorities;

    b. identify gaps in, and barriers to, protection;

    c. seek to close gaps in protection through appropriate and effectively coordinated schemes, whether contributory or non-contributory, or both, including through the extension of existing contributory schemes to all concerned persons with contributory capacity;

    d. complement social security with active labour market policies, including vocational training or other measures, as appropriate;

    e. specify financial requirements and resources as well as the time frame and sequencing for the progressive achievement of the objectives; and

    f. raise awareness about their social protection floors and their extension strategies, and undertake information programmes, including through social dialogue.

15. Social security extension strategies should apply to persons both in the formal and informal economy and support the growth of formal employment and the reduction of informality, and should be consistent with, and conducive to, the implementation of the social, economic and environmental development plans of Members.

16. Social security extension strategies should ensure support for disadvantaged groups and people with special needs.

17. When building comprehensive social security systems reflecting national objectives, priorities and economic and fiscal capacities, Members should aim to achieve the range

and levels of benefits set out in the Social Security (Minimum Standards) Convention, 1952 (No. 102), or in other ILO social security Conventions and Recommendations setting out more advanced standards.

18. Members should consider ratifying, as early as national circumstances allow, the Social Security (Minimum Standards) Convention, 1952 (No. 102). Furthermore, Members should consider ratifying, or giving effect to, as applicable, other ILO social security Conventions and Recommendations setting out more advanced standards.

IV. MONITORING

19. Members should monitor progress in implementing social protection floors and achieving other objectives of national social security extension strategies through appropriate nationally defined mechanisms, including tripartite participation with representative organizations of employers and workers, as well as consultation with other relevant and representative organizations of persons concerned.

20. Members should regularly convene national consultations to assess progress and discuss policies for the further horizontal and vertical extension of social security.

21. For the purpose of Paragraph 19, Members should regularly collect, compile, analyse and publish an appropriate range of social security data, statistics and indicators, disaggregated, in particular, by gender.

22. In developing or revising the concepts, definitions and methodology used in the production of social security data, statistics and indicators, Members should take into consideration relevant guidance provided by the International Labour Organization, in particular, as appropriate, the resolution concerning the development of social security statistics adopted by the Ninth International Conference of Labour Statisticians.

23. Members should establish a legal framework to secure and protect private individual information contained in their social security data systems.

24.

1. Members are encouraged to exchange information, experiences and expertise on social security strategies, policies and practices among themselves and with the International Labour Office.

2. In implementing this Recommendation, Members may seek technical assistance from the International Labour Organization and other relevant international organizations in accordance with their respective mandates.

Annex 2: Sustainable Development Goals related to social protection

Goal 1
End poverty in all its forms everywhere
Target 1.3
Implement nationally appropriate social protection systems and measures for all, including floors, and by 2030 achieve substantial coverage of the poor and the vulnerable

Goal 3
Ensure healthy lives and promote well-being for all at all ages
Target 3.8
Achieve universal health coverage, including financial risk protection, access to quality essential health-care services and access to safe, effective, quality and affordable essential medicines and vaccines for all

Goal 5
Achieve gender equality and empower all women and girls
Target 5.4
Recognize and value unpaid care and domestic work through the provision of public services, infrastructure and social protection policies and the promotion of shared responsibility within the household and the family as nationally appropriate

Goal 8
Promote sustained, inclusive and sustainable economic growth, full and productive employment and decent work for all
Target 8.5
By 2030, achieve full and productive employment and decent work for all women and men, including for young people and persons with disabilities, and equal pay for work of equal value

172. Universal Schemes

Goal 10
Reduce inequality within and among countries
Target 10.4
Adopt policies, especially fiscal, wage and social protection policies, and progressively achieve greater equality

Annex 3: ILO standards on social protection

The up-to-date ILO Conventions and Recommendations on social security or social protection are listed below:

- The Social Security (Minimum Standards) Convention, 1952 (No. 102), which covers all nine branches of social security and sets minimum standards for these nine branches;
- The Income Security Recommendation, 1944 (No. 67) and the Medical Care Recommendation, 1944 (No. 69), which envisage comprehensive social security systems and the extension of coverage to all and laid the foundations for Convention No. 102 (1952).
- The Social Protection Floors Recommendation (No. 202) provides guidance for the establishment and maintenance of social protection floors and their implementation within strategies for the extension of social security aiming at achieving comprehensive social security system.

Other up-to-date Conventions and Recommendations, adopted after Convention No. 102 (1952), set out higher standards for particular branches of social security. Drawn up on the model of Convention No. 102, they offer a higher level of protection, both in terms of the population covered and of the level of benefits, as follows:

- The Medical Care and Sickness Benefits Convention, 1969 (No. 130) and the Medical Care and Sickness Benefits Recommendation, 1969 (No. 134) makes provision for medical care and sickness benefit;
- The Employment Promotion and Protection against Unemployment Convention, 1988 (No. 168) and the Employment Promotion and Protection against Unemployment Recommendation, 1988 (No. 176) relates to unemployment benefit;

- The Invalidity, Old-Age and Survivors' Benefits Convention, 1967 (No. 128) and the Invalidity, Old-Age and Survivors' Benefits Recommendation, 1967 (No. 131) covers old-age benefit, invalidity benefit and survivor's benefit;
- The Employment Injury Benefits Convention, 1964 (No. 121) and the Employment Injury Benefits Recommendation, 1964 (No. 121) makes provision for employment injury benefit;
- The Maternity Protection Convention, 2000, (No. 183) and the Maternity Protection Recommendation, 2000 (No. 191) covers maternity benefit;
- The Equality of Treatment (Social Security) Convention, 1962 (No. 118), the Maintenance of Social Security Rights Convention, 1982 (No. 157) and the Maintenance of Social Security Rights Recommendation, 1983 (No. 167) provide reinforced protection to migrant workers; and

These instruments can be consulted in the Database of International Labour Standards. (NORMLEX)